THE COOKING FOR ONE COOKBOOK

THE
COOKING
FOR ONE
COOKBOOK

100
EASY RECIPES

CINDY KERSCHNER

PHOTOGRAPHY BY LAURA FLIPPEN

ROCKRIDGE
PRESS

Cover Recipe: Margherita Buddha Bowl, Page 46
Interior and Cover Designer: Diana Haas
Photo Art Director: Sara Feinstein
Editor: Jesse Aylen
Production Editor: Gleni Bartels
Photography © 2019 Laura Flippen. Food Styling by Laura Flippen.
Author photo courtesy of © Troy Schnyder.

ISBN: Print 978-1-64152-984-6 | eBook 978-1-64152-985-3
R0

Thanks to Margaret, James, and Maureen,
who stood by me and shared their solo cooking tips,
recipes, and techniques over the years.

CONTENTS

INTRODUCTION

THE COOKING FOR ONE COOKBOOK challenges and encourages solo cooks to engage with their kitchens to craft simple, satisfying, and convenient meals. Whether you're a novice or a more "seasoned" cook, in these pages you'll find a wide array of recipes to fit easily into your day. Cooking meals at home has so many benefits; you control the ingredients, prep time, portions, and cost. On a deeper level, cooking your food builds a connection between you and what you put into your body. It's a connection that lets us keep the unfortunate surprises out and the delicious flavor in.

My passion for food began in childhood. Mom and I planted a vegetable garden with green beans, onions, peppers, and carrots, and I helped weed and harvest. My favorite dinner began with picking fresh green beans for Mom's ham and string bean soup. Mom provided a succinct lesson in portion control by handing me a one-quart saucepan, instructing me to fill it to the top. That simple request guaranteed our family a fresh supply of green beans for our dinner—not too much and not too little—and it meant that we would have vegetables waiting for our next meal.

When I first moved out on my own, I was determined to make those dishes Mom taught me. After all, a little comfort food goes a long way! I incorporated her ideas for portioning each item per serving, and for me, that meant lower costs and less food waste. It's a lesson that has aged well, since scaling recipes for one is a strategy I use to this day on my blog, *Cindy's Recipes and Writings*.

But before you move to the recipes, we'll discuss furnishing your "cooking for one" kitchen. The first chapter covers the basic pots, pans, and utensils needed to make cooking for one convenient and efficient, and I'll share my tips on how to stock your pantry for ready access to foods you'll need on hand regularly.

Most importantly, this cookbook features 100 easy-to-make recipes designed to be budget- and time-friendly. Over three-quarters of the recipes can be made from start to finish in 30 to 45 minutes or less, making them perfect for college students, single adults, and busy seniors.

I've structured these recipes around weekly meal plans intended to alleviate food-related stress, so you'll find a two-week sample meal plan to make scheduling even easier.

With both a day's food and a book, it's important to start at the beginning. A quick breakfast is the right way to "break" what's literally been a "fast," and chapter 2, Easy Breakfasts for One, gives you 15 accessible recipes to begin your day with the fuel you need. Short on time? Don't stress! Many of these dishes can be taken on the go.

Lunch often takes a backseat in our busy lives. Promising yourself to grab something later often results in a wilted convenience-store salad, but packing lunch guarantees a true midday boost. There are several recipes in chapter 3, Lunch Made Easy, to make and take along for a healthy meal. One of my favorites, BBQ Chicken Shaker Salad, offers a fresher, wallet-friendly alternative to prepackaged salads, and it's unbelievably simple to make.

Lastly, preparing dinner doesn't have to be overwhelming or time-consuming. In fact, cooking simple dinners can be an effective way to save time and money, and reinforces that soulful connection between your body and your food. The Meatless Mains for One chapter will stir your cravings for a meat-free meal, with choices like Roasted Vegetable Lasagna and Spicy Black-Eyed Peas and Rice. Chapter 5, One if by Sea, brings 15 ways to enjoy the catch of the day. Shrimp and Crab Cakes, Pesto Salmon, and Seafood Creole recipes are each ready in under 30 minutes. In chapter 6, Proteins Made Simple, you'll find inventive ways to use chicken, beef, pork, and turkey in tried-and-true recipes like Chicken Piccata, a lively Pork Chop with Pineapple Salsa, and smoky Chipotle Rib Eye.

The last chapter, Treat Yourself, is a full array of desserts for one. Chocolate lovers can dig into a Cinnamon Chocolate Brownie or take a bite of velvety Mocha Fudge. Those with a fruitier dessert palate should try the Apple Kugel or a juicy Berry Galette.

The recipes include tips intended to be tailored to your needs and tastes. Some recipes include shortcuts, while others offer key ingredient nutritional information to boost your culinary know-how. You'll find substitutions to help replace missing ingredients, and flavorful options to switch up the taste profiles and keep you happy, healthy, and satisfied.

My sincere hope is that you come to enjoy and rely on *The Cooking for One Cookbook* as much as I have enjoyed bringing it to you! Happy cooking, and even happier eating!

Grocery
List
· vanilla
· mixed berries
· sugar
· pie crust
· eggs
· lemons
· basil
· Kalamata olives
· plum tomatoes

CHAPTER ONE

THINKING SOLO AND SHOPPING SMART: KITCHEN BASICS AND MEAL PLANNING FOR ONE

Helpful Kitchen Equipment for One

Every cook needs basic equipment to get the job done, and having the right saucepans, skillets, griddles, and essentials at the ready will make cooking solo at home easy and affordable. A reliable kitchen, boosted by a thoughtfully well-stocked pantry, is all you need to start.

KITCHEN ESSENTIALS

1-QUART AND 2-QUART SAUCEPANS WORK FOR MOST RECIPES. A 1-quart saucepan is useful for crafting sauces, cooking grains, and reheating. A 2-quart saucepan works best for simmering soups, boiling vegetables, and making pasta.

SAUTÉ PANS OR SKILLETS THAT ARE HEAVY DUTY AND OVEN SAFE. Using these reliable pans for chicken, steaks, and chops keeps the meat juicy and tender. I use my 10-inch, medium sauté pan for most meals, proving its endless usefulness.

A NONSTICK GRIDDLE WILL GO A LONG WAY IN MEAL PREP for items like eggs, pancakes, sandwiches, and burgers.

BAKING PANS (ALSO CALLED SHEET PANS OR BAKING SHEETS) ARE MULTIPURPOSE. A standard-size 9x13-inch sheet pan offers a place to roast vegetables or toast nuts for healthy add-ons. Many one-pan meals can be cooked directly on a high-quality sheet pan.

MUFFIN PANS AND RAMEKINS WORK GREAT FOR BAKING. For making desserts, muffins, and individual snacks, 7- or 8-ounce ramekins handle those tasks with ease.

GOOD KNIVES ARE YOUR MOST IMPORTANT KITCHEN TOOL. A basic knife set includes three standard knives. Use a paring knife for precise cuts. A chef's knife will efficiently cut vegetables and herbs and thinly slice cheeses. A serrated knife works best for bread and cooked meat.

DIGITAL THERMOMETERS GUIDE YOU IN COOKING and reheating to the proper temperatures, and assure food safety.

CUTTING BOARDS LIMITED TO PARTICULAR INDIVIDUAL USES, like preparing vegetables or raw meat, prevent cross-contamination from meats and poultry into other foods.

PROPER MEASURING TOOLS CAN MAKE OR BREAK A RECIPE, especially when it comes to baking. Purchase separate graduated dry and liquid measuring cup sets. Measuring spoons take the guesswork out of portions. A good set for the solo cook includes a ⅛ teaspoon, ¼ teaspoon, ½ teaspoon, 1 teaspoon, ½ tablespoon, and 1 tablespoon. A ⅛ teaspoon can be filled halfway for 1/16 teaspoon or "dash" requirements in a recipe.

HEAT-RESISTANT UTENSILS SERVE A DUAL PURPOSE FOR STOVETOP AND OVEN USE. Spatulas, whisks, tongs, and stirring and slotted spoons will cover most of your cooking needs. Consider purchasing a fish spatula, as its thin blade comes in handy when transferring delicate fish.

HOT PADS, POT HOLDERS, OR OVEN MITTS ARE A MUST. Safety first! Keep some of each kind on hand.

A COLANDER FOR DRAINING, WASHING, AND RINSING SAVES TIME. It's one of my favorite multipurpose tools.

BASIC KITCHEN APPLIANCES to consider investing in include a blender for smoothies, sauces, dressings, and even chopping ice; and a mini food processor for grating or mincing vegetables.

PANTRY STAPLES FOR ONE

Wouldn't it be satisfying to go to a grocery store and find your entire shopping list in one aisle? A well-stocked home pantry is the equivalent, as it saves time, money, and effort.

BUY DRIED HERBS INDIVIDUALLY. Use basil, thyme, oregano, rosemary, parsley, and dill individually, or create your own customized blends. Rosemary, thyme, oregano, and garlic powder make a great homemade Italian seasoning. Store these mixes for several months in airtight containers.

STOCK A VARIETY OF SALTS. Salts to keep on hand include kosher, sea, and table salt. Coarse salt is great for seasoning rubs and is super easy to sprinkle. Table salt works best for salting cooking water and for baking recipes, and it's referred to as "salt" throughout this book's recipes.

HAVE A VARIETY OF PEPPER IN THE PANTRY. Peppercorns are great freshly ground or added whole to soups and stews. Paprika and crushed red pepper flakes add zing to many dishes.

MAINTAIN A CACHE OF BASIC DRY BAKING NEEDS. A combination of all-purpose flour, granulated sugar, brown sugar, baking powder, and baking soda make the base for countless cookies, cakes, and breads.

KEEP GOOD FATS ON HAND, including vegetable oil and olive oil. Used sparingly, butter adds rich flavor and helps in browning. Vegetable oil and olive oil are essential in cooking, baking, and crafting salad dressings.

A TOUCH OF ACID BRIGHTENS MOST DISHES. Red wine, apple cider, and white vinegar are good cupboard staples. When refrigerated, lemon or lime juice concentrate keeps for several months.

DRIED PASTA AND RICE MAKE EASY MAIN DISHES AND SIDES. Spaghetti, elbows, and shells are my go-to pasta shapes. Use them alone with sauce, or add protein and vegetables to create delicious casseroles. White and brown rice can be made ahead, portioned, and frozen to use as needed.

CANNED GOODS HAVE THEIR PLACE. I like to keep tomato sauce and paste, plus canned beans, to grab for quick sauces and meals.

Shopping Solo: Handy Tips and Tricks

Shopping for groceries does not have to be a chore, especially if planned in advance. Meal planning helps remove the stress from what to make and how much to buy. Buying the right quantities for the week's meals cuts back not only on food waste, but also on unnecessary expenditure. Because you won't be overwhelmed with leftovers, what you do have on hand can be easily repurposed.

BUYING FOR ONE

There's no doubt that buying for one can be a challenge! Here are a few inventive tips to help you get the most out of your shopping trip.

CHECK STORE FLYERS. Before shopping, check in-store flyers and online offers. Sometimes you can find price cuts for meal-plan items you often use, but hadn't planned to buy at that moment.

GET TO KNOW THE BUTCHER AT YOUR STORE'S MEAT COUNTER. Find smaller steaks with help from the butcher; cuts of rib eye, strip, or sirloin are often not displayed, or are kept apart for ground beef that's made in-store. Don't be afraid to ask for them!

SEEK OUT SINGLE-SERVING POUCHES. Individual pouches of tuna or salmon make easy lunch sandwiches and salads. These portions are ideal as the building-block inspiration for simple recipes.

YOUR FREEZER CAN BE YOUR BEST HELPER. Buying meat in bulk, like chicken breasts or pork chops, may seem intimidating, yet it's always priced more equitably. Portion chicken for later use by wrapping pieces individually in plastic wrap and storing in one resealable freezer bag. Label and date the bag with month and day to ensure nothing stays for too long before being used.

USE FROZEN SHRIMP AS A GREAT QUICK-MEAL OPTION. Buy a one-pound bag and keep it handy in the freezer. Thaw the portion as needed for your recipe. Choose medium-size shrimp (21 to 25 count) for the most versatile use.

BUY FROZEN BAGS OF VEGETABLE MEDLEYS. Buy extra vegetables, like peppers and onions, as medleys. Great to have on hand, these vegetable blends add flavor and nutrients to stir-fries, omelets, soups, and stews.

CHOOSE READY-CUT GREENS. Buy ready-cut bagged lettuce to use for single-serve salads. To ensure remaining lettuce doesn't go to waste, think beyond the salad bowl and use it for burgers, tacos, sandwiches, and more.

BUY THE SMALLEST PACK OF FRESH HERBS AVAILABLE. Buy small packs ranging from ¼ to ¾ ounces. Meal-plan to use basil, thyme, or rosemary for more than one meal. Thyme, rosemary, parsley, and oregano freeze well. You can chop fresh parsley or cilantro before freezing it, and later use the chopped herbs straight from the freezer.

REPURPOSE LEFTOVER CANNED BEANS TO MAKE GREAT HUMMUS. Add some lemon, tahini, and garlic for standard hummus, easily whipped up in your food processor.

CREATE MEAL-PLAN RECIPES TO USE MULTIUSE VEGETABLES. Buy a five-pound (or less) bag of multipurpose potatoes to cover several recipes in your week's meal plan. From breakfast potatoes to lunchtime fresh-cut fries and dinner mashed potatoes alongside your main dish, there are easy ways to finish that bag before the potatoes spoil.

SHOPPING FOR ONE

Get creative when food shopping time hits with these solo-sized tips.

THINK OUTSIDE THE BOX (STORE) WHEN IT COMES TO FOOD SHOPPING. Most larger stores are geared to family-size portions and packaging. Look for stores that offer fresh meat and seafood counter sales. These direct-sale spaces will have someone to help you decide which tuna steak or rib eye to buy and can also tailor portions to your needs.

YOUR COUNTY COOPERATIVE EXTENSION SERVICE OFFICE CAN HELP. You'll likely find farm stands, farmers markets, meat markets, dairies, and local co-ops in your area. Search for their contact information online or in the blue pages of directory lists.

DON'T STRESS OVER GETTING EVERYTHING IN ONE TRIP. Focus on which ingredients you need most. You can divide purchases into weekly or biweekly shopping trips according to your meal plan and make substitutions where needed.

A Deliciously Easy Two-Week Plan

It's so easy to fall into a rut when it comes to cooking for one. When I was young, my mother's meal plan was steadfastly based on the day of the week, and with predictability came boredom. Monday was inevitably chicken, while Wednesday unquestionably meant spaghetti. Whether you like an unwavering schedule or prefer to mix it up, meal planning for one should be both thoughtful *and* satisfying. Structuring your meals makes shopping and food prep easier on both your schedule and budget and lets you get excited for what's to come.

Meal plans are also a great way to reimagine leftovers into new dishes. The meal plan here includes tasty repurposing opportunities, like saving leftover Orange-Maple Smoked Pork Chops from Sunday to reinterpret for Monday's Ham and Potato Breakfast Hash.

Flexible by design, this two-week meal plan is a solid place to get started. It incorporates a variety of techniques and healthy meal choices, not to mention delectable desserts. Read ahead in the week before you start cooking, because often leftovers from one day will be repurposed for another meal. While the titled recipes are listed in the book, you'll find them complemented by simple-to-prepare accompaniments that guarantee your meal will be deliciously well rounded.

Week One

SUNDAY

Breakfast: Apple Crumb French Toast

Lunch: Grilled Chicken Club Sandwich

Dinner: Orange-Maple Smoked Pork Chop, garlic mashed potatoes, grilled asparagus

Dessert: Vanilla Mug Cake

MONDAY

Breakfast: Ham and Potato Breakfast Hash (using leftover Orange-Maple Smoked Pork Chop)

Lunch: Corn, Chickpea, and Orzo Salad with Chicken (using leftover grilled chicken from Grilled Chicken Club Sandwich)

Dinner: Roasted Vegetable Lasagna, garlic bread (see tip in Fisherman's Stew, page 83), Caesar salad

Dessert: Apple Kugel (using leftover apples from Apple Crumb French Toast filling)

TUESDAY

Breakfast: Blueberry Oatmeal Pancakes

Lunch: Roasted Vegetable Quesadilla (using leftover roasted vegetables from Roasted Vegetable Lasagna)

Dinner: Sausage and Peppers, multigrain rice pilaf, steamed broccoli

Dessert: Raisin Bread Pudding

WEDNESDAY

Breakfast: Farmers Market Greens Smoothie

Lunch: Chickpea and Tomato Salad, whole-wheat crackers

Dinner: Coffee-Rubbed Steak, baked potato, green beans

Dessert: Cranberry Rice Pudding

THURSDAY

Breakfast: Steak and Egg Breakfast Cups (using leftover Coffee-Rubbed Steak), fresh fruit cup with yogurt (using leftover fruit from Farmers Market Greens Smoothie)

Lunch: Margherita Buddha Bowl (using leftover tomatoes from Chickpea and Tomato Salad)

Dinner: Easy Fish and Chips, tossed garden salad

Dessert: No-Bake Blueberry Cheesecake
(Note: Prepare Overnight Strawberry Oatmeal for tomorrow's breakfast.)

FRIDAY

Breakfast: Overnight Strawberry Oatmeal

Lunch: Cod with Pico de Gallo (using leftover fish from Easy Fish and Chips)

Dinner: Buffalo Tofu Pasta Bake, dill carrots

Dessert: Berry Galette with vanilla ice cream

SATURDAY

Breakfast: Very Berry Breakfast Parfaits (using leftover berries and oatmeal from Overnight Strawberry Oatmeal)

Lunch: Alaskan Salmon Burger, tortilla chips with pico de gallo (using leftover salsa from Cod with Pico de Gallo)

Dinner: Mushroom Stroganoff, sautéed sugar snap peas

Dessert: Mini Strawberry Graham Pies with Greek yogurt

Week Two

SUNDAY

Breakfast: Mushroom and Spinach Quiche

Lunch: Cuban Pitas, carrot and celery sticks

Dinner: Beef-and-Shrimp Surf and Turf, twice-baked potato, steamed broccoli

Dessert: Cinnamon Chocolate Brownie

MONDAY

Breakfast: Ham and Potato Breakfast Hash

Lunch: Hot Ham-and-Cheese Sliders (using leftover ham from Cuban Pitas), spinach side salad, apple slices

Dinner: Beef Barley Skillet Dinner (using leftover beef from Beef-and-Shrimp Surf and Turf), steamed asparagus with lemon

Dessert: Chocolate Chip Cookie Bar

TUESDAY

Breakfast: Brussels Sprouts and Potato Patties, scrambled eggs

Lunch: Turkey Monte Cristo, tomato cucumber salad

Dinner: Shrimp-and-Crab Cakes (using leftover shrimp from Beef-and-Shrimp Surf and Turf), broccoli slaw

Dessert: Pumpkin Pie with whipped cream

WEDNESDAY

Breakfast: Spicy Breakfast Burrito (using leftover scrambled eggs)

Lunch: Lemon-Dill Shrimp Salad, bed of greens salad

Dinner: Hickory BBQ Chicken Legs, macaroni salad, sauteed kale with garlic

Dessert: Peanut Butter Pie

THURSDAY

Breakfast: Peachy Smoothie Bowl, Corn Muffins

Lunch: Avocado and Black Bean Tostada, small arugula side salad

Dinner: Seafood Creole (using leftover shrimp and crabmeat from Shrimp-and-Crab Cakes)

Dessert: Chocolate Chip Mug Cake (Vanilla Mug Cake with added chocolate chips)

FRIDAY

Breakfast: Malted Chocolate Energy Bites, soft boiled egg, hash browns (using leftover Brussels Sprouts and Potato Patties)

Lunch: BBQ Chicken Shaker Salad (using leftover chicken from the Hickory BBQ Chicken Legs), cinnamon-sugar tortilla chips (see tip in Avocado and Black Bean Tostadas, page 33)

Dinner: Pesto Salmon, buttered noodles, oven-roasted cauliflower

Dessert: Cookies-and-Cream Cake

SATURDAY

Breakfast: Homemade Granola with almond milk, fresh fruit cup

Lunch: Creamy Pesto Chicken Salad over greens (using leftover greens and pesto from Pesto Salmon)

Dinner: Garden Burger, smashed potatoes, roasted Brussels sprouts

Dessert: Piña Colada Blondie

MUSHROOM AND SPINACH
QUICHE, PAGE 23

CHAPTER TWO

EASY BREAKFASTS FOR ONE

Breakfast is not a meal to skip, as tempting as that may be in the morning rush. It provides the fuel your body needs to face a busy day. Still, a nutritious breakfast doesn't need to be boring, because the right balance of protein, fats, and carbohydrates can take many forms. Easy eggs, fruity oatmeal crisps, whole-grain muffins, and nourishing smoothies are power-packed with fruits and vegetables to kick-start your morning, whether you're enjoying a leisurely one or having a grab-and-go start!

Apple Crumb French Toast

YIELD: 2 SLICES / PREP TIME: 10 MINUTES / COOK TIME: 20 MINUTES

MAKE AHEAD, NUT FREE, QUICK MEAL

The comforting flavors of apple, combined with cinnamon, hearty oats, and a touch of cayenne, will entice any palate. To introduce different textures, try swapping the white bread for wheat, challah, or sourdough.

4 tablespoons unsalted butter, divided

1 apple, cored, peeled, and chopped (such as Gala, Fuji, or McIntosh)

1 teaspoon cinnamon, divided

1 tablespoon lemon juice

1 teaspoon plus 2 tablespoons brown sugar, divided

⅛ teaspoon cayenne pepper

1 large egg

2 tablespoons reduced-fat (2-percent) milk

½ teaspoon vanilla extract

½ teaspoon granulated sugar

2 slices white bread

¼ cup rolled oats

1 tablespoon all-purpose flour

1. Preheat a small sauté pan or skillet over medium heat. Melt 1 tablespoon butter in pan. Add the apple, ½ teaspoon cinnamon, lemon juice, 1 teaspoon brown sugar, and cayenne pepper. Cook for about 10 minutes, stirring occasionally, until apples are soft and liquid forms a syrup. Remove the pan from the heat and cover to keep warm.

2. Preheat a medium sauté pan over medium-low heat. Melt 1 tablespoon butter.

3. In a small mixing bowl, whisk together the egg, milk, vanilla, and sugar. Dip both sides of the bread in the egg mixture, and place slices in the heated pan. Sprinkle each slice with about ¼ teaspoon cinnamon. Fry bread until firm and golden brown, flip, and continue cooking until the second side is golden brown, 3 to 4 minutes per side.

4. Heat a small sauté pan over medium heat. Melt remaining 2 tablespoons butter. Add the oats, remaining 2 tablespoons brown sugar, and flour. Cook over medium heat, stirring constantly until the oats are lightly browned. Remove from the heat.

5. Place French toast on a serving plate. Spoon on apple topping and sprinkle on crumbs.

Reheat Tip: Reheat frozen French toast slices in a toaster at the lowest setting.

Per serving: Calories: 874; Total Fat: 54g; Saturated Fat: 32g; Cholesterol: 311mg; Sodium: 441mg; Carbohydrates: 86g; Fiber: 6g; Protein: 14g

Blueberry Oatmeal Pancakes

YIELD: 3 PANCAKES / PREP TIME: 15 MINUTES / COOK TIME: 5 MINUTES

MAKE AHEAD, NUT FREE, QUICK MEAL

To pump up the volume on a breakfast staple, this recipe marries the delicate taste and health benefits of oats with the sweetness of honey. Don't forget to allow the mixed batter to sit—it's valuable time that gives the gluten an opportunity to expand and guarantees fluffier pancakes.

¼ cup all-purpose flour

¼ cup rolled oats

½ teaspoon baking powder

⅛ teaspoon salt

½ cup low-fat buttermilk

1 large egg, beaten

1 teaspoon vegetable oil

1 tablespoon honey

½ teaspoon vanilla extract

Cooking spray

¼ cup blueberries, fresh or frozen

1. In a food processor, grind the flour, oats, baking powder, and salt until coarsely ground. Place the mixture in a medium mixing bowl.

2. In a separate small mixing bowl, whisk together the buttermilk, egg, vegetable oil, honey, and vanilla. Fold the wet ingredients into the dry ingredients, mixing until just combined. Allow the batter to rest for 5 to 10 minutes, without stirring.

3. Heat a griddle or medium sauté pan sprayed with cooking spray over medium-high heat for 1 minute. Drop ½ teaspoon of the batter to test if the pan is hot enough. The test droplet should sizzle, but not burn. If the droplet burns, lower the temperature. Pour ¼ cup batter for each pancake. Sprinkle with blueberries. When bubbles form in the batter, flip the pancake, about 2 minutes. Continue frying the second side until golden brown, about 2 to 3 minutes.

4. Test by inserting toothpick, which will come out clean when pancake is cooked.

Solo Storage Tip: Freeze by stacking cooled pancakes with a sheet of wax paper between each in a resealable plastic freezer bag. Reheat in the microwave until completely reheated.

Per serving: Calories: 410; Total Fat: 12g; Saturated Fat: 3g; Cholesterol: 191mg; Sodium: 494mg; Carbohydrates: 61g; Fiber: 3g; Protein: 15g

Brussels Sprouts and Potato Patties

YIELD: 2 PATTIES / PREP TIME: 15 MINUTES / COOK TIME: 10 MINUTES

DAIRY FREE, MAKE AHEAD, NUT FREE, VEGAN

I grew up eating potato patties made with leftover mashed potatoes. While they're undeniably a classic, we can modernize them by using shredded potatoes, while high-fiber Brussels sprouts contribute depth and vitamins.

1 medium potato, skin on and shredded

¼ cup shredded Brussels sprouts

2 tablespoons minced yellow onion

¼ teaspoon kosher salt

⅛ teaspoon freshly ground black pepper

1 tablespoon all-purpose flour, divided into 3 teaspoons

1 tablespoon vegetable oil

1. In a colander, rinse the shredded potato for about 2 minutes, stirring the shreds by hand to release starch. Wrap the drained shredded potatoes in paper towels and gently squeeze out any excess water.

2. In a large mixing bowl, mix the potatoes, Brussels sprouts, onion, salt, and pepper. Mix in 1 teaspoon of flour at a time, until the mixture binds together. Divide the mixture in half, gently patting each ball into a patty about ½-inch thick.

3. Heat a medium sauté pan or griddle over medium heat for about 1 minute. Add the vegetable oil to the pan and heat until it shimmers. Place patties gently, frying until browned, about 5 minutes. Flip each patty when it easily lifts loose with a spatula, cooking about 5 minutes more. Drain the cooked patties on a paper towel to remove any excess grease.

Substitution Tip: Punch up these portable breakfast treats by adding shredded carrots or diced broccoli to the mix.

Per serving: Calories: 334; Total Fat: 14g; Saturated Fat: 1g; Cholesterol: 10mg; Sodium: 169mg; Carbohydrates: 47g; Fiber: 6g; Protein: 6g

Cheesy Breakfast Grits

YIELD: 1 CUP / PREP TIME: 10 MINUTES / COOK TIME: 10 MINUTES

5 INGREDIENTS OR FEWER, GLUTEN FREE, NUT FREE, QUICK MEAL

My first grits experience was the luscious combination of shrimp and grits, and it was love at first bite! Grits are so versatile, it's hard to find a topping that *doesn't* work. Try adding bacon bits, green bell pepper, or green onion.

1 cup water

⅛ teaspoon kosher salt

¼ cup quick-cook grits

2 tablespoons part-skim shredded Cheddar cheese

1. In a 1-quart saucepan over medium heat, bring the water and salt to a boil. Slowly pour in grits to avoid splashing hot liquid. Reduce the heat to medium-low. Stir constantly while cooking to avoid grits sticking to the pan.

2. Cook grits over medium-low heat for 5 to 7 minutes, until they reach the consistency of mashed potatoes. Remove the pan from the heat. Spoon into a serving bowl. Stir in the cheese until completely melted.

Variation Tip: For a sweeter morning start, omit the cheese, add berries or peaches, and swirl honey through to brighten the dish.

Per serving: Calories: 169; Total Fat: 2g; Saturated Fat: 1g; Cholesterol: 3mg; Sodium: 162mg; Carbohydrates: 31g; Fiber: 1g; Protein: 7g

Corn Muffins

YIELD: 6 MUFFINS / PREP TIME: 10 MINUTES / COOK TIME: 20 TO 25 MINUTES

GOOD FOR LEFTOVERS, MAKE AHEAD, NUT FREE

What's better than a warm corn muffin with a bit of butter? It's a light grab-and-go breakfast that satisfies hunger while packing key nutrients like vitamin C and magnesium. While this recipe includes stone-ground cornmeal for more texture than regular, softer cornmeal, feel free to use either.

½ cup all-purpose flour

½ cup yellow stone-ground cornmeal

¼ cup granulated sugar

2 teaspoons baking powder

½ teaspoon kosher salt

½ cup whole milk

1 large egg, lightly beaten

2 tablespoons unsalted butter, melted

1. Preheat oven to 425°F.
2. Line 6 compartments of a cupcake pan with paper liners or grease lightly with vegetable shortening. In a medium mixing bowl, whisk together the flour, cornmeal, sugar, baking powder, and salt. In a separate small mixing bowl, mix together milk, egg, and melted butter.
3. Fold half of the wet ingredients into the dry mixture using a rubber or plastic spatula until the wet ingredients are absorbed. Repeat with remaining wet ingredients.
4. Using a tablespoon, fill the prepared cups about ⅔ full with batter. Bake for 20 to 25 minutes, or until muffins are golden brown and a toothpick inserted in the center comes out clean. To avoid crumbling, cool the pan on a cooling rack for 5 minutes before moving muffins to a cooling rack.

Variation Tip: Create cornbread stuffing with leftover muffins. Crumble 2 muffins into a microwave-safe bowl. In a small sauté pan over medium heat, melt 1 tablespoon butter and sauté 1 tablespoon diced celery and 1 tablespoon diced onion for 1 minute, or until just softened. Add 2 tablespoons chicken broth. Pour over the muffin crumbles, then heat in the microwave for about 1 minute, until warmed through.

Per serving (1 muffin): Calories: 167; Total Fat: 6g; Saturated Fat: 3g; Cholesterol: 43mg; Sodium: 100mg; Carbohydrates: 26g; Fiber: 1g; Protein: 4g

Farmers Market Greens Smoothie

YIELD: 2 CUPS / PREP TIME: 5 MINUTES

MAKE AHEAD, NO BAKE, ONE POT, QUICK MEAL

Try blending fresh spinach, baby kale, carrots, honey, and banana with yogurt and milk for a delicious, nutritious on-the-go meal. I like my smoothies with almond milk for a slightly nutty taste and velvety texture. Go rogue and experiment with different fruits and veggies to create your own perfectly custom mix.

½ cup nonfat yogurt

½ banana, peeled and halved

⅓ cup milk (2-percent, soy, or almond)

½ cup fresh baby spinach

½ cup fresh baby kale

½ cup peeled and chopped carrots

1 teaspoon honey

2 tablespoons orange juice

1 cup ice

Combine the yogurt, banana, milk, spinach, kale, carrots, honey, orange juice, and ice in a blender. Pulse to roughly chop. Then increase the speed to purée the ingredients until smooth. Serve immediately, or pour into an insulated portable cup.

Preparation Tip: Keep calories down by using lower-sugar juices. Check the labels on nut milks for fat and added sugar content.

Per serving: Calories: 245; Total Fat: 2g; Saturated Fat: 1g; Cholesterol: 9mg; Sodium: 220mg; Carbohydrates: 47g; Fiber: 4g; Protein: 13g

Ham and Potato Breakfast Hash

YIELD: 2 CUPS / PREP TIME: 10 MINUTES / COOK TIME: 45 MINUTES

BAKE AND SERVE, DAIRY FREE, GLUTEN FREE, ONE POT

Conquer your morning by cracking an egg on this hearty hash and letting the yolk run down into this universally popular comfort food. As a bonus, this one-pan meal requires little cleanup and can be made vegetarian by eliminating the ham.

1 large skin-on red potato, diced

½ small sweet potato, peeled and diced (about ½ cup)

½ cup diced fully cooked ham

¼ teaspoon kosher salt

⅛ teaspoon freshly ground black pepper

1 tablespoon extra-virgin olive oil

Cooking spray

¼ cup diced green bell pepper

¼ cup diced yellow onion

1 large egg

1. Preheat oven to 375°F.
2. Put the red potatoes, sweet potatoes, ham, salt, ground pepper, and olive oil in a resealable plastic bag. Shake to coat the potatoes thoroughly. Spray a baking sheet with cooking spray. Spread the bag contents out evenly onto the baking sheet. Bake for 15 minutes, or until the potatoes and ham are lightly browned. Using an oven-safe spatula, flip the potato and ham pieces over.
3. Sprinkle the bell peppers and onions evenly throughout. Roast for an additional 10 to 15 minutes, or until the peppers are soft and onions are translucent.
4. Crack an egg carefully into a small bowl, so as not to break the yolk. Gently pour the egg near the center of the baking sheet. Cook the egg to the desired degree of doneness: soft, medium, or extra firm.
5. Before eating, break the yolk with a fork and mix it into the hash, if desired.

Preparation Tip: For this recipe, I recommend a large egg, which takes about 10 minutes to cook. The whites will be firm and the egg will retain a runny yolk.

Per serving: Calories: 637; Total Fat: 25g; Saturated Fat: 6g; Cholesterol: 224mg; Sodium: 1,160mg; Carbohydrates: 80g; Fiber: 10g; Protein: 26g

Homemade Granola

YIELD: 2 CUPS / PREP TIME: 10 MINUTES / COOK TIME: 45 MINUTES

DAIRY FREE, GLUTEN FREE, GOOD FOR LEFTOVERS, MAKE AHEAD

Take a break from ordinary cereals and try homemade granola. To make this recipe vegan, substitute maple syrup for honey and serve with almond milk.

1 cup rolled oats

1 tablespoon brown sugar

⅛ teaspoon kosher salt

1 tablespoon raw sunflower seeds or roasted pumpkin seeds

2 tablespoons canola oil

1 tablespoon honey

¼ cup dried fruit (one type or a combination of raisins, cranberries, apricots, apples)

1 tablespoon toasted sliced almonds

1. Preheat oven to 300°F.
2. Line a baking pan with parchment paper. In a medium mixing bowl, combine the oats, brown sugar, salt, and seeds.
3. In a separate small bowl, stir together the canola oil and honey. Using a rubber spatula, stir the oil and honey into the oats. Spread the granola in an even, single layer on the lined baking pan.
4. Bake, stirring after about 20 minutes with a heat-resistant rubber spatula.
5. Continue baking until the granola is light golden brown, about 25 minutes more. Granola will harden as it cools. Remove the baking pan from the oven and place on a cooling rack. Stir in the dried fruit and toasted almonds. Loosen the cooked granola by hand as it cools. Store cooled granola in an airtight container for up to 1 week.

Variation Tip: Go tropical by substituting coconut oil for canola oil. Omit seeds and use chopped dried pineapple or mango. As the granola cools, stir in 1 tablespoon sweetened shredded coconut.

Per serving (1 cup): Calories: 409; Total Fat: 19g; Saturated Fat: 2g; Cholesterol: 0mg; Sodium: 45mg; Carbohydrates: 57g; Fiber: 5g; Protein: 7g

Malted Chocolate Energy Bites

YIELD: 6 PIECES / PREP TIME: 5 MINUTES / CHILL TIME: 15 MINUTES

MAKE AHEAD, NO BAKE

While the peanut butter and hemp seeds in these energy-packed bites add protein, the cocoa and chocolate amp up the antioxidants. Rounding it all out with a touch of sweetness, honey adds to the energy boost with healthy carbs that are easy for your body to digest.

⅓ cup creamy peanut butter

½ cup rolled oats

½ cup hemp seeds or flax seeds

1 tablespoon honey

1 teaspoon Dutch-processed or natural cocoa powder

1 tablespoon malted milk powder

½ cup semisweet chocolate chips

1. In a medium mixing bowl, stir together the peanut butter and oats until creamy and well mixed. Add the seeds, honey, cocoa powder, malted milk powder, and chocolate chips. Stir until evenly distributed. The mixture will be sticky. Refrigerate for at least 15 minutes, so it will be easier to portion and form into bites.

2. Roll the chilled mixture into 6 bite-size balls. Store in an airtight container in the refrigerator for up to one week.

Substitution Tip: Add a crunch with some toasted sweetened coconut. Preheat the oven to 300°F. Spread ¼ cup sweetened coconut as a single layer on a baking sheet. Bake, stirring often, for about 10 minutes until coconut is light brown. Work the toasted coconut a little bit at a time into the dough before portioning it into balls, or roll the portioned balls in toasted coconut.

Per serving (1 piece): Calories: 279; Total Fat: 16g; Saturated Fat: 5g; Cholesterol: 0mg; Sodium: 71mg; Carbohydrates: 27g; Fiber: 4g; Protein: 8g

Mushroom and Spinach Quiche

YIELD: 1 SERVING / PREP TIME: 15 MINUTES / COOK TIME: 50 MINUTES

BAKE AND SERVE, GOOD FOR LEFTOVERS, NUT FREE

This simple quiche nestles the meaty texture of portobello mushrooms and creamy eggs inside a flaky crust. Serve with a fruit salad for a complete breakfast or brunch!

½ prepared refrigerator pie dough

1 teaspoon vegetable oil

¼ cup chopped portobello mushrooms

½ cup chopped fresh baby spinach

2 large eggs

1 tablespoon reduced-fat (2-percent) milk

1. Preheat oven to 450°F.
2. Gently press the dough into an ungreased 7-ounce oven-safe ramekin, starting at the bottom and working up the sides to the top of the container. Using a paring knife, trim the dough evenly with the top of the ramekin. Using a fork, score the bottom and sides of the dough. Fold a 1-inch piece of aluminum foil in half lengthwise and place it loosely over the top of the ramekin to prevent the crust from overbaking. Bake on a baking sheet for 15 minutes, or until the crust is golden brown. Remove the baking sheet to a heat-resistant surface.
3. Heat a small sauté pan over medium heat for about 1 minute. Add the oil and heat until it shimmers. Fry the mushrooms in the pan over medium heat until the mushrooms are evenly browned and softened. Remove from the heat and add the spinach, stirring to combine.
4. In a small mixing bowl, whisk together the eggs and milk. Stir in the mushrooms and spinach. Pour the egg mixture into the prepared crust, level with the top of the ramekin.
5. Bake the quiche on the baking sheet for 30 minutes, or until a fork inserted into the custard comes out clean. Remove the top crust foil and bake for about 5 minutes longer to brown the top of quiche. Place the ramekin on a cooling rack for about 5 minutes before serving.

Substitution Tip: Swap in chopped broccoli and fresh tomatoes for the mushrooms and spinach for a new take.

Per serving: Calories: 523; Total Fat: 36g; Saturated Fat: 7g; Cholesterol: 273mg; Sodium: 558mg; Carbohydrates: 34g; Fiber: 1g; Protein: 17g

Overnight Strawberry Oatmeal

YIELD: 1 CUP / PREP TIME: 10 MINUTES / CHILL TIME: 5 TO 8 HOURS

5 INGREDIENTS OR FEWER, MAKE AHEAD, NO BAKE, VEGAN

When prepared the night before, this treat is ready to go in the morning when you are. Take it on the road or enjoy it at home with your coffee. The oats, with all of their health benefits, combine with fresh fruit and milk to create a beautifully balanced meal.

½ cup rolled oats, divided

¼ cup sliced fresh strawberries, divided

½ cup almond milk

1. In an 8-ounce glass, 1-cup mason jar, or resealable container, layer ¼ cup oats topped with 2 tablespoons strawberries. Repeat, layering with remaining ¼ cup oats and 2 tablespoons strawberries.
2. Pour almond milk over the top, covering the oats completely.
3. Cover with plastic wrap and refrigerate for at least 5 hours before eating. For best results, refrigerate for 8 hours. Stir before eating. Overnight oats are best enjoyed within two days after preparation.

Variation Tip: If you prefer warm oatmeal, microwave finished overnight oats in a microwave-safe container on high for 10-second intervals until thoroughly heated.

Per serving: Calories: 246; Total Fat: 9g; Saturated Fat: 0g; Cholesterol: 0mg; Sodium: 265mg; Carbohydrates: 32g; Fiber: 7g; Protein: 8g

Peachy Smoothie Bowl

YIELD: 2 CUPS / PREP TIME: 10 MINUTES

NO BAKE, QUICK MEAL

A variation on the expected smoothie, Peachy Smoothie Bowls let your creativity shine. Offset with a bit of crunch on top from pepitas (roasted pumpkin seeds), and other creative additions like chopped nuts, sunflower seeds, or granola, peaches are the star of this dish. Simply start by blending yogurt with fruit and juice, and experiment with different fruits and seeds to find your favorite version.

1 cup fresh (1 large peach) or frozen peach slices, divided

½ cup nonfat Greek yogurt (plain or vanilla)

2 tablespoons orange juice

¼ cup almond milk

¼ cup loose granola

1 tablespoon pepitas or sunflower seeds

1 tablespoon hemp heart seeds or chia seeds

1. In a blender, add ½ cup peaches, yogurt, orange juice, and almond milk. Pulse to chop peaches to desired consistency. Switch speed to purée for 20 to 30 seconds to blend.

2. Pour the smoothie mixture into an individual serving bowl. Arrange remaining ½ cup peaches, granola, pepitas or sunflower seeds, and hemp heart or chia seeds in rows on top.

Substitution Tip: Make your smoothie bowl nondairy by exchanging the yogurt for ½ ripe banana. For more protein, add peanut butter, almond butter, or cashew butter before blending.

Per serving: Calories: 283; Total Fat: 9g; Saturated Fat: 2g; Cholesterol: 5mg; Sodium: 112mg; Carbohydrates: 38g; Fiber: 9g; Protein: 18g

Spicy Breakfast Burrito

YIELD: 1 BURRITO / PREP TIME: 10 MINUTES / COOK TIME: 25 MINUTES

QUICK MEAL

This recipe starts with scrambled eggs, peppers, onions, cheese, and ground beef before adding zippy jalapeños. For a vegetarian swap, beans make a tasty and filling alternative.

1 teaspoon vegetable oil

⅓ cup lean ground beef (85 percent lean)

½ teaspoon taco seasoning

1 tablespoon diced yellow onion

1 tablespoon diced green bell pepper

2 large eggs, beaten

1 10-inch flour tortilla

2 tablespoons prepared salsa (or see Cod with Pico de Gallo, page 80)

¼ jalapeño pepper, diced, seeds and membrane removed

2 tablespoons shredded part-skim Cheddar cheese

¼ teaspoon hot sauce (optional)

Cooking spray

1. Heat a small sauté pan over medium heat for about 1 minute. Add the oil and heat until it shimmers. Add the ground beef, taco seasoning, onion, and bell peppers to the pan. Fry, stirring occasionally, until the ground beef is thoroughly cooked and the peppers and onions are soft, about 10 minutes.

2. Pour the eggs over the mixture. Cook over medium heat, stirring constantly, until the eggs are cooked, about 5 minutes.

3. Microwave the tortilla between two damp paper towels for 20 seconds to soften. Spoon the beef mixture onto the center of the tortilla, spreading evenly and leaving a 2-inch border around the tortilla edge for folding.

4. Spoon the salsa and jalapeño over the meat mixture. Sprinkle with the cheese. Add hot sauce, if using. Fold the tortilla over the filling by first folding the sides toward the center. Fold the bottom up toward the center. Roll away from you, tucking in exposed tortilla corners to close.

5. Lightly spray a griddle or medium sauté pan with cooking spray. Heat the pan over medium-high heat until the spray shimmers, about 2 minutes. Place the burrito seam-side down. Cook, turning on all sides, over medium-high heat to brown and melt cheese, about 5 minutes.

Substitution Tip: For a leaner breakfast, replace the ground beef with ground chicken or turkey.

Per serving: Calories: 660; Total Fat: 35g; Saturated Fat: 11g; Cholesterol: 414mg; Sodium: 1174mg; Carbohydrates: 49g; Fiber: 3g; Protein: 37g

Steak and Egg Breakfast Cups

YIELD: 2 / PREP TIME: 10 MINUTES / COOK TIME: 20 MINUTES

BAKE AND SERVE, MAKE AHEAD, QUICK MEAL

Try this modern twist on a 1950s classic breakfast staple. These even work without the steak! Make them lighter by using fresh chopped green vegetables like spinach, kale, and broccoli instead of steak. No matter what you choose, using a bit of cheese in these egg breakfast cups makes them filling *and* indulgent.

1 teaspoon vegetable oil

½ ounce beef minute steak or shaved beef

2 teaspoons minced yellow onion

2 teaspoons minced green bell pepper

2 large eggs

1 tablespoon reduced-fat (2-percent) milk

⅛ teaspoon kosher salt

⅛ teaspoon freshly ground black pepper

Cooking spray

1 tablespoon part-skim shredded Cheddar cheese

1. Preheat oven to 350°F.
2. In a small sauté pan, heat the oil over medium heat until it shimmers, about 2 minutes. Sauté the steak, onion, and bell pepper until the steak is thoroughly cooked and vegetables are tender, about 2 to 3 minutes. Set aside.
3. In a small mixing bowl, beat together the eggs, milk, salt, and pepper. Set aside. Spray 2 compartments of a cupcake pan with cooking spray. Divide the egg mixture between the two greased compartments. Place half of the steak and half of the cheese into each compartment. Do not stir, as stirring may cause egg cups to stick. Bake for 15 minutes, or until inserted toothpick comes out clean.

Variation Tip: If you like a rarer steak option, use finely chopped precooked rarer steak and add it after the vegetables are cooked.

Per serving: Calories: 302; Total Fat: 17g; Saturated Fat: 4g; Cholesterol: 298mg; Sodium: 287mg; Carbohydrates: 21g; Fiber: 3g; Protein: 20g

Very Berry Breakfast Parfaits

YIELD: 1 CUP / PREP TIME: 5 MINUTES

5 INGREDIENTS OR FEWER, NO BAKE, QUICK MEAL

Customizable and fun, parfaits are the perfect breakfast treat for one. They've become ubiquitous, but don't buy a less-than-fresh option at a corner grocery when you can make it at home. When it comes to the granola layer, either purchase loose granola or prepare Homemade Granola in advance.

½ cup plain or vanilla low-fat yogurt, divided

½ cup mixed fresh berries (raspberries, chopped strawberries, blueberries), divided

¼ cup loose granola (or Homemade Granola, page 21)

1. In an 8-ounce glass, 1-cup mason jar, or resealable container, layer ¼ cup yogurt and top with ¼ cup berries.

2. Repeat, layering with remaining ¼ cup yogurt and ¼ cup berries. Top with granola.

Variation Tip: For an even sweeter treat, try adding 1 tablespoon chocolate chips and shredded sweetened coconut to the granola.

Per serving: Calories: 165; Total Fat: 3g; Saturated Fat: 2g; Cholesterol: 7mg; Sodium: 93mg; Carbohydrates: 23g; Fiber: 2g; Protein: 9g

LEMON-DILL SHRIMP SALAD, PAGE 45

CHAPTER THREE

LUNCH MADE EASY

Whether you're a packer or a midday cook, lunch is your chance to take a break, reboot your energy, and enjoy something delicious and healthy. It is also an excellent opportunity to repurpose leftovers and make inventive use of previously purchased ingredients, like in this chapter's BBQ Chicken Shaker Salad, Tuscan Bean Soup, and Alaskan Salmon Burger. With these recipes, apportioned just right for one and sensibly timed for a hectic life, you won't be sacrificing quality *or* flavor.

Alaskan Salmon Burger

YIELD: 1 BURGER / PREP TIME: 10 MINUTES / CHILL TIME: 15 MINUTES / COOK TIME: 20 MINUTES

GOOD FOR LEFTOVERS, MAKE AHEAD, NUT FREE

Heart-healthy salmon, either canned or in easy-to-use pouches, makes great burgers for a quick lunch. Don't stress about finding fresh salmon if your schedule is tight; use any cooked flaked salmon. I've added a truly regional twist; a former colleague of mine reported that many burgers in Alaska come with a fried egg on top for added protein and energy in a chilly climate. Cold weather or not, it's one tasty lunchtime addition.

3 ounces flaked and cooked salmon, skin removed

2 large eggs, 1 egg beaten for patty, 1 egg whole for frying

2 tablespoons mayonnaise, divided

¼ teaspoon dry mustard

½ teaspoon lemon juice

¼ teaspoon seafood seasoning, divided

½ cup panko bread crumbs, divided

1 tablespoon vegetable oil

Cooking spray

1 kaiser roll or hamburger bun, toasting optional

1. In a medium mixing bowl, combine the salmon, beaten egg, 1 tablespoon mayonnaise, dry mustard, lemon juice, and ⅛ teaspoon seafood seasoning. Stir in the panko, 1 tablespoon at a time, to form a moist mixture. Shape into a patty by hand and coat it with reserved bread crumbs, gently turning until evenly coated. Refrigerate the patty for 15 minutes before frying.

2. Place a small sauté pan over medium heat, add oil, and heat until it shimmers, about 1 minute. Fry the patty until golden brown, turning once, about 2 to 3 minutes per side. Transfer to a plate, and cover with foil to keep warm.

3. Spray a small sauté pan with cooking spray, and place over medium heat. Add the whole egg and cook until the egg white is firm (for sunny-side-up egg) or flip and cook about 1 minute longer (for an over-easy egg). Assemble the burger on the bun, then top with the fried egg. Mix the remaining 1 tablespoon mayonnaise with remaining ⅛ teaspoon seafood seasoning. Spread the top bun with seasoned mayonnaise.

Substitution Tip: To switch up the flavor, try flaked tuna or canned crabmeat instead.

Per serving: Calories: 734; Total Fat: 44g; Saturated Fat: 7g; Cholesterol: 439mg; Sodium: 792mg; Carbohydrates: 44g; Fiber: 3g; Protein: 40g

Avocado and Black Bean Tostadas

YIELD: 1 SANDWICH / PREP TIME: 15 MINUTES / COOK TIME: 10 MINUTES

ONE POT, QUICK MEAL

Mexican-inspired flavors rule this deliciously layered yet deceptively simple meal. Tostada ("toasted") refers to the way a tortilla is prepared. Tostadas are typically deep-fried flat, or in a bowl shape, before being crowned with meat and toppings. My lighter version bakes the tortilla to a satisfying crisp, skips the meat, and adds lush and creamy avocado.

1 (6-inch) flour or corn tortilla

1 tablespoon vegetable oil

2 tablespoons canned or homemade refried beans

¼ cup shredded lettuce

¼ cup canned black beans, rinsed and drained

½ plum tomato, chopped

1 tablespoon diced green onion (green and white parts mixed)

½ avocado, sliced

Juice of ½ lime

1 tablespoon shredded part-skim Cheddar cheese

Sour cream (optional)

1. Preheat oven to 400°F.

2. Place the tortilla on a baking sheet. Lightly brush both sides of the tortilla with oil. Bake the tortilla for 3 to 5 minutes per side, or until crisp. Use tongs to move the finished tostada shell from the oven to a plate.

3. Using a wooden spoon or plastic spatula, spread the tostada shell with a thin coating of refried beans. Sprinkle the shredded lettuce over the refried beans. Spoon on black beans, tomato, green onion, and avocado slices, and drizzle with lime juice. Sprinkle with cheese. Serve with sour cream, if desired.

Variation Tip: For a quick treat, tortillas can be easily turned into a sweet snack. Preheat oven to 350°F. Cut the tortilla into quarters to make 4 equal pieces. Brush both sides lightly with butter, then sprinkle with cinnamon and sugar. Arrange quarters in a single layer on a baking sheet, then bake for 8 to 10 minutes until crisp.

Per serving: Calories: 462; Total Fat: 31g; Saturated Fat: 5g; Cholesterol: 10mg; Sodium: 164mg; Carbohydrates: 40g; Fiber: 14g; Protein: 12g

BBQ Chicken Shaker Salad

YIELD: 2 CUPS / PREP TIME: 10 MINUTES

NO BAKE, ONE POT, QUICK MEAL

BBQ Chicken Shaker Salad is a great way to shake things up—literally. In this crunchy salad, ranch dressing pairs perfectly with the tang of the barbecue chicken. Even prepared in advance, this salad will remain crisp and ready for lunchtime if you use some creative layering.

1 cup cooked chicken breast, diced

¼ cup barbecue sauce, homemade (see Hickory BBQ Chicken Legs, page 109) or purchased

2 tablespoons low-fat ranch dressing

1 small tomato, chopped

1 cup shredded leaf or romaine lettuce

1 tablespoon bacon bits

¼ cup diced carrots

¼ cup diced broccoli

¼ cup garlic croutons

1. In a small mixing bowl, combine the cooked chicken and barbecue sauce. Set aside.
2. Layer the ingredients into a pint-size mason jar, starting with the dressing. Spoon the ranch dressing into the bottom of the jar. In even layers, add the chicken, tomatoes, lettuce, bacon bits, carrots, broccoli, and croutons. Close the lid tightly and refrigerate until ready for use.
3. When ready to eat, shake the jar until all the ingredients are thoroughly coated with dressing, about 30 seconds to 1 minute. Eat the salad directly from the jar or pour it onto serving plate.

Variation Tip: Try a lighter, homemade version of ranch dressing made with tangy yogurt. In a small mixing bowl, stir together 1 cup nonfat Greek yogurt, ¼ cup low-fat buttermilk, ⅛ teaspoon kosher salt, ⅛ teaspoon onion powder, and ⅛ teaspoon garlic powder until evenly combined.

Per serving: Calories: 571; Total Fat: 18g; Saturated Fat: 4g; Cholesterol: 129mg; Sodium: 1,405mg; Carbohydrates: 43g; Fiber: 3g; Protein: 54g

Cheesy Beef Chili

YIELD: 2 CUPS / PREP TIME: 15 MINUTES / COOK TIME: 30 MINUTES

GLUTEN FREE, ONE POT

Rumor has it that chili first sprung to popularity at the Chicago World's Fair. This recipe, like the original, offers the same belly-warming feel owing to its hearty combination of steak, roasted poblano pepper, and other Southwestern-style spices. Be careful when steam-loosening the pepper skin and finely dicing the pepper. While it is a bit of a more intensive step, you're sure to love the smoky flavor the broiled pepper brings. To bulk up the dish, add any leftover beans and chopped vegetables from your refrigerator.

1 tablespoon vegetable oil

4 ounces steak (such as sirloin or top round), cut into bite-size pieces

¼ cup diced yellow onion

½ fresh roasted poblano pepper, diced

2 tablespoons unsalted tomato paste

½ cup unsalted beef broth

½ teaspoon chili powder

¼ teaspoon smoked paprika

½ cup diced fresh tomatoes

½ teaspoon fresh cilantro, chopped

⅛ teaspoon kosher salt

2 tablespoons part-skim shredded cheese

1. Heat a medium sauté pan over medium-high heat for about 1 minute. Add the oil to the pan and heat until it shimmers, about 1 minute. Add the steak and onion, stirring occasionally until the steak is browned, about 8 to 10 minutes for medium rare, or 10 to 12 minutes for medium. Reduce heat to low to keep the cooked steak warm.

2. Heat the broiler on high for about 2 minutes. Place the poblano pepper skin-side up on a baking sheet. Broil it about 4 inches under the broiler element with the oven door slightly open for 3 to 4 minutes, or until the skin blisters and blackens. Using tongs, move the pepper to a paper bag, or wrap it in paper towels to retain heat, which will steam-loosen the skin. Let the pepper rest for 5 minutes, then carefully scrape off the skin with a paring knife, and dice the pepper. Add the diced pepper to the steak.

3. In a medium mixing bowl, whisk together the tomato paste, beef broth, chili powder, and smoked paprika until combined. Stir in the diced tomatoes, cilantro, and salt, then add the sauce to the steak. Stir to distribute the sauce evenly.

CONTINUED ▸

4. Heat the chili in the same pan over medium-low heat for about 5 minutes, stirring until thoroughly heated. Stir the cheese into the chili until the cheese has melted. Spoon the chili into a serving bowl.

Variation Tip: For a warming vegan option, substitute your favorite beans for beef, swap low-sodium vegetable broth for beef broth, and omit the cheese.

Per serving: Calories: 454; Total Fat: 35g; Saturated Fat: 10g; Cholesterol: 100mg; Sodium: 236mg; Carbohydrates: 7g; Fiber: 2g; Protein: 27g

Chickpea and Tomato Salad

YIELD: 1 CUP / PREP TIME: 10 MINUTES / COOK TIME: 25 MINUTES

DAIRY FREE, GOOD FOR LEFTOVERS, NUT FREE, QUICK MEAL, VEGAN

Chickpeas are a great plant-based protein and source of fiber, folate, and iron. Teamed with juicy tomatoes, which add vitamins A and C to the mix, this lunch is a virtual multivitamin in a bowl. Roasting the tomatoes both brings out their natural sweetness and allows the salad's spices and seasonings to blend in with the juices.

½ cup grape or cherry tomatoes, halved

2 tablespoons extra-virgin olive oil, divided

½ teaspoon minced garlic

½ teaspoon dried basil

¼ teaspoon dried oregano

¼ teaspoon kosher salt

1 cup canned garbanzo beans (chickpeas), rinsed and drained

2 teaspoons lemon juice

½ teaspoon granulated sugar

1 teaspoon fresh basil, chopped

1. Preheat oven to 400°F.
2. In a small bowl, combine tomatoes, 1 tablespoon olive oil, garlic, basil, oregano, and salt. Pour the tomato mixture onto a baking pan, spreading in an even, single layer. Roast for 20 to 25 minutes, or until the tomatoes begin to caramelize, soften, and turn lighter in color. Remove the baking pan from the oven and cool at room temperature for 10 minutes.
3. In a small mixing bowl, mix the roasted tomatoes and chickpeas with a spatula.
4. In a second small mixing bowl, whisk together the remaining 1 tablespoon olive oil, lemon juice, sugar, and fresh basil. Pour the dressing over the salad and fold to coat evenly. Serve immediately, or chill in the refrigerator for at least 30 minutes.

Variation Tip: Leftover Chickpea and Tomato Salad makes a vibrant pasta sauce. Put the salad in a food processor and pulse until smooth. If the sauce is too thick, add a drizzle of extra-virgin olive oil to thin it out.

Per serving: Calories: 540; Total Fat: 33g; Saturated Fat: 5g; Cholesterol: 0mg; Sodium: 168mg; Carbohydrates: 52g; Fiber: 14g; Protein: 16g

Creamy Pesto Chicken Salad

YIELD: 1 CUP / PREP TIME: 15 MINUTES

NUT FREE, ONE POT

This homemade pesto is quick to make, has no need for a mortar and pestle, and can be used on a variety of dishes like pasta, rice, shrimp, and grilled vegetables. To make it creamier, add a bit of mayonnaise or sour cream. To thin it out, add an extra touch of extra-virgin olive oil.

½ cup fresh basil leaves, stems removed

1 small garlic clove

¼ cup grated Parmesan cheese

2 teaspoons extra-virgin olive oil

¼ teaspoon kosher salt (optional)

½ cup mayonnaise

1 cup shredded cooked chicken breast

1. In a food processor, pulse the basil, garlic, and Parmesan cheese until finely chopped. With food processor running, drizzle the olive oil into the food processor to form a loose paste.
2. Scrape the pesto into a small mixing bowl with a spatula. Taste the pesto before adding salt. Stir in additional salt if needed. Fold the mayonnaise into the pesto until completely mixed.
3. Place the chicken in a small bowl and stir in enough pesto to moisten, a tablespoon at a time. Serve as a stand-alone meal, a tossed-salad topping, or a sandwich filling.

Variation Tip: Add 1 tablespoon of pistachios to the pesto for extra protein and texture, just pulse together with the basil, garlic, and cheese.

Per serving: Calories: 839; Total Fat: 69g; Saturated Fat: 14g; Cholesterol: 153mg; Sodium: 759mg; Carbohydrates: 2g; Fiber: 0g; Protein: 50g

Corn, Chickpea, and Orzo Salad

YIELD: 1 CUP / PREP TIME: 10 MINUTES / COOK TIME: 10 MINUTES

GOOD FOR LEFTOVERS, MAKE AHEAD, QUICK MEAL, VEGAN

This salad makes a nourishing vegan meal you can prepare ahead of time for an easy grab-and-go lunch. Traditionally used in soups, orzo pasta now takes prime place in this lively salad, which also contains chickpeas that boost the protein, fiber, and LDL (the "good") cholesterol. A hint of basil rounds out the salad beautifully.

Cooking spray

¼ cup frozen corn

¼ cup canned garbanzo beans (chickpeas), rinsed and drained

½ cup cooked orzo

1 teaspoon minced red bell peppers

¼ teaspoon minced garlic

½ teaspoon minced red onion

1 teaspoon lemon juice

1 tablespoon extra-virgin olive oil

⅛ teaspoon kosher salt

¼ teaspoon dried basil

1. Preheat oven to 350°F.
2. Spray a baking sheet with cooking spray and arrange the corn in a single layer. Roast for 5 to 10 minutes, or until the corn begins to brown, stirring occasionally to avoid sticking. Remove the pan and place it on a cooling rack for about 10 minutes.
3. In a medium mixing bowl, stir together the cooled corn, chickpeas, orzo, bell peppers, garlic, and onion.
4. In a separate bowl, whisk together lemon juice, olive oil, salt, and basil. Drizzle the salad with dressing and stir to coat.

Variation Tip: Extra chickpeas make a great roasted snack. Preheat the oven to 400°F. Dry the chickpeas on paper towels. Using 1 tablespoon of vegetable oil per cup of chickpeas, toss the chickpeas and spread them in a single layer onto a parchment-lined baking sheet. Roast for 30 to 40 minutes until crisp, stirring occasionally. Toss roasted chickpeas with a light sprinkling of kosher salt.

Per serving: Calories: 314; Total Fat: 16g; Saturated Fat: 2g; Cholesterol: 0mg; Sodium: 105mg; Carbohydrates: 39g; Fiber: 6g; Protein: 8g

Cuban Pitas

YIELD: 1 SANDWICH / PREP TIME: 10 MINUTES / MARINATING TIME: 30 MINUTES / COOK TIME: 10 MINUTES

MAKE AHEAD, NUT FREE, ONE POT

My Cuban Pitas preserve the classically layered taste of this sandwich, but save time. Rather than using traditional slow-roasted pork, marinate cooked pork in brown sugar, cumin, citrus, and paprika. Layer this sandwich just so for an authentic taste: first mustard, then ham, then pickles, then pork, then Swiss cheese. This thoughtful combination will mix salt, sweet, sour, and zesty in one bite!

2 teaspoons extra-virgin olive oil

2 teaspoons orange juice

½ teaspoon lime juice

1 teaspoon brown sugar

½ teaspoon kosher salt

¼ teaspoon smoked paprika

¼ teaspoon ground cumin

¼ teaspoon garlic powder

½ cup cooked, sliced or shredded pork tenderloin

1 teaspoon yellow mustard

1 pita bread, cut in half

1 slice deli ham

1 small sliced kosher pickle

1 slice Swiss cheese

Cooking spray

1. In a medium mixing bowl, whisk together the olive oil, orange juice, lime juice, brown sugar, salt, smoked paprika, cumin, and garlic powder until the brown sugar is dissolved. Place the pork and marinade into a 1-quart resealable bag. Toss to coat. Let the pork marinate in the refrigerator for at least 30 minutes.

2. Spread mustard on one half of the pita. Top it with ham, pickle slices, pork, and Swiss cheese. Place the other pita half on top.

3. Lightly spray a medium sauté pan with cooking spray, and place over medium-low heat. Placing the pita carefully to preserve the layered ingredients, fry on both sides until lightly browned and the Swiss cheese has melted, about 5 minutes per side.

Cooking Tip: Marinate the pork overnight. The longer the pork sits in the marinade, the more the flavors will intensify.

Per serving: Calories: 521; Total Fat: 23g; Saturated Fat: 8g; Cholesterol: 88mg; Sodium: 1,255mg; Carbohydrates: 43g; Fiber: 3g; Protein: 35g

Deviled Egg Salad

YIELD: 1 CUP / PREP TIME: 10 MINUTES / COOK TIME: 15 MINUTES

GOOD FOR LEFTOVERS, GLUTEN FREE, NUT FREE, QUICK MEAL

These devilishly delicious bites can be made in various ways, but almost always begin with eggs, mayonnaise, and tangy mustard. In this take on the cocktail-party classic, brown mustard contributes a bit of spice, while red wine vinegar adds tang. Served atop tossed greens, as a sandwich filling, or simply by itself, this dish makes enough egg salad for two meals, guaranteeing that it's doubly worth your time.

½ teaspoon salt

4 large eggs

1 tablespoon mayonnaise

1 teaspoon brown mustard

½ teaspoon red wine vinegar

⅛ teaspoon garlic powder

⅛ teaspoon kosher salt

1. Fill a 1-quart saucepan with cold water to about an inch from the top. Add salt to the water. Gently place the eggs in the cold water. Add additional cold water to cover the eggs as necessary. Over medium heat, bring the water to a boil. Once the water begins to boil, set a timer for 12 minutes. Boil eggs on a gentle boil to avoid cracking. Remove the pan from the heat. Run cold water over the eggs to cool.

2. Peel the cooled eggs and chop them into ¼-inch pieces. In a small mixing bowl, mix chopped eggs, mayonnaise, mustard, vinegar, garlic powder, and salt with a plastic spatula. Serve as a salad or sandwich filling.

Variation Tip: For a heartier and tangier version, stir chopped green olives or chopped sweet pickles into the finished salad.

Per serving: Calories: 378; Total Fat: 30g; Saturated Fat: 8g; Cholesterol: 749mg; Sodium: 1,528mg; Carbohydrates: 2g; Fiber: 0g; Protein: 25g

Garlic Tofu Cobb Salad

YIELD: 1 SERVING / PREP TIME: 15 MINUTES, PLUS 2 HOURS REFRIGERATION AND PRESSING TIME / COOK TIME: 10 MINUTES

GLUTEN FREE, NUT FREE

Fried tofu pairs perfectly with eggs, avocado, and feta in this twist on the classic Cobb salad. One crucial piece of advice: Don't forget to press the tofu. Remove excess liquid before cooking by placing the tofu slices (cut to one-inch thickness) between paper towels and adding a slightly heavier item on top to weigh it down. For best results, refrigerate the pressed tofu for two hours.

Cooking spray

2 ounces pressed extra firm tofu

1 teaspoon garlic powder, divided

½ teaspoon kosher salt, divided

⅛ teaspoon freshly ground black pepper, divided

1 hard-boiled egg, chopped

1 plum tomato, chopped

½ avocado, sliced

¼ cup crumbled blue cheese or feta

1 cup spring lettuce mix

3 tablespoons extra-virgin olive oil

2 tablespoons red wine vinegar

¼ teaspoon oregano

¼ teaspoon minced garlic

1. Heat a griddle or small sauté pan sprayed with cooking spray over medium heat until it shimmers, about 1 minute. Season the tofu with ½ teaspoon garlic powder, ¼ teaspoon salt, and dash of pepper. Fry over medium heat until browned and firm on both sides, about 5 minutes per side.

2. Arrange the tofu, egg, tomato, avocado, and cheese on top of spring lettuce.

3. In a small mixing bowl, whisk together olive oil, vinegar, oregano, garlic, and remaining garlic powder, salt, and pepper. Drizzle dressing over salad.

Substitution Tip: Try other meatless substitutes like tempeh or seitan to mix up this Cobb. Made with fermented soy, tempeh has a firmer texture than tofu and easily absorbs flavors, while seitan is wheat-based with a firm, meat-like texture.

Per serving: Calories: 790; Total Fat: 71g; Saturated Fat: 15g; Cholesterol: 189mg; Sodium: 589mg; Carbohydrates: 18g; Fiber: 9g; Protein: 24g

Grilled Chicken Club Sandwich

YIELD: 1 SANDWICH / PREP TIME: 10 MINUTES / COOK TIME: 15 MINUTES

DAIRY FREE, NUT FREE, QUICK MEAL

One of my first jobs was at a traditional family-owned deli where I had my first exposure to triple-decker sandwiches. While theirs was a classic club with bacon, tomato, and lettuce, my more modern take replaces the expected ham and turkey with tender, and leaner, white-meat chicken.

1 teaspoon vegetable oil

1 (4-ounce) chicken breast fillet, thinly sliced or pounded to ¼-inch thickness

⅛ teaspoon kosher salt

⅛ teaspoon freshly ground black pepper

1 large piece leaf lettuce

3 slices toasted bread of your choice

1 slice cooked bacon

2 slices tomato

1 teaspoon mayonnaise

1. Heat the oil in a small sauté pan over medium-high, until it shimmers, about 1 minute. Season the chicken breast with salt and pepper, and add the chicken to pan.

2. Fry the chicken over medium-high heat for about 5 minutes on the first side until the chicken browns and easily loosens (without tearing) from the pan. Reduce heat to medium, flip the chicken with tongs, and cook for 7 to 10 minutes, or until browned and the internal temperature reaches 165°F.

3. Build the sandwich by placing lettuce on the bottom of the toasted bread, topped with chicken. Add another toast slice, then layer the bacon and tomato. Spread mayonnaise on the remaining slice of bread. Place the last slice, mayonnaise-side down, over the tomato. Toothpick the sandwich on all four corners along the crust. Cut diagonally. Gently lift each segment, pushing the toothpick through to hold the layers together.

Variation Tip: Feeling like a bit of spice? Add a few drops of hot sauce to the mayonnaise or season the chicken with a dash of cayenne and smoked paprika.

Per serving: Calories: 619; Total Fat: 29g; Saturated Fat: 6g; Cholesterol: 113mg; Sodium: 1,074mg; Carbohydrates: 37g; Fiber: 6g; Protein: 51g

Hot Ham-and-Cheese Sliders

YIELD: 3 SLIDERS / PREP TIME: 10 MINUTES / COOK TIME: 10 MINUTES

MAKE AHEAD, NUT FREE, QUICK MEAL

Hot Ham-and-Cheese Sliders are a whimsical way to enjoy a classic. Making it mini makes it more fun, especially because you get to eat more than just one! Slider rolls are available in most supermarkets and even from smaller bakeries. Ham brings a salty component balanced nicely by the zesty, sweet honey mustard sauce, but don't be afraid to flex the ingredients and find your new custom reimagined slider.

Cooking spray

1 tablespoon unsalted butter

3 slider rolls

¼ pound sliced deli ham (3 to 4 slices)

3 slices American or Cheddar cheese, cut diagonally

1 teaspoon honey

2 teaspoons Dijon mustard

1 teaspoon mayonnaise

1. Spray a griddle or medium sauté pan with cooking spray, and heat over medium-low heat until it shimmers, about 1 minute. Spread butter onto the rolls and fry, buttered-side down, for 3 minutes, checking often so the bread does not burn. Set toasted rolls aside.

2. In the same pan, fry the ham over medium heat in 3 separate, even stacks for 5 minutes, turning as needed until the ham browns evenly. Arrange 2 cheese triangles over each pile of ham. Reduce heat to low and allow the cheese to melt without burning the ham. Stack on the prepared buns.

3. In a small mixing bowl, combine the honey, mustard, and mayonnaise. Spread the mustard dressing on the rolls. Add the ham and melted cheese to the buns, and serve warm.

Variation Tips: Experiment to find your favorite ham for this sandwich. Some flavored variations to try include peppered ham, capicola, Black Forest, or turkey ham for a lighter bite. To up the spice, add a slick of hot sauce to the rolls along with the honey mustard.

Per serving: Calories: 891; Total Fat: 55g; Saturated Fat: 30g; Cholesterol: 184mg; Sodium: 1,704mg; Carbohydrates: 54g; Fiber: 3g; Protein: 46g

Lemon-Dill Shrimp Salad

YIELD: 1 CUP / PREP TIME: 20 MINUTES / COOK TIME: 10 MINUTES

DAIRY FREE, GLUTEN FREE, GOOD FOR LEFTOVERS, NUT FREE, QUICK MEAL

One of the most versatile and low-calorie proteins, shrimp plays nicely with the lemon, oil, dill, and spices in this refreshing salad. When preparing for this meal, I buy two-pound bags of frozen shrimp and thaw specific portions as needed. While this recipe suggests steaming the shrimp, it can also be panfried in roughly the same amount of time.

1 cup raw medium shrimp, peeled and deveined

2 tablespoons extra-virgin olive oil

1 teaspoon lemon juice

¼ teaspoon lemon zest

¼ teaspoon dried dill

¼ teaspoon Dijon mustard

⅛ teaspoon granulated sugar

1 cup baby arugula or baby spinach

1. In a 2-quart saucepan, steam the shrimp by covering it halfway with water, then covering the pan with a lid. Bring the water to a boil over medium heat; boil for about 1 minute. Reduce the heat to low and simmer the shrimp about 2 minutes. Turn off the burner. Allow the shrimp to stand, covered, for an additional 1 to 2 minutes, until pink and opaque.

2. In a medium mixing bowl, whisk together the olive oil, lemon juice, lemon zest, dill, mustard, and sugar. Fold in the cooked shrimp with a rubber spatula and stir to coat.

3. Place arugula or spinach on a serving plate. Top with the prepared shrimp salad. Serve warm or chill for later use. Cold olive oil dressings will appear cloudy, but resume proper consistency when they warm to room temperature.

Variation Tip: Make leftovers into a pasta sauce. Roughly chop the salad in a food processor, adding olive oil as needed to thin out the chopped shrimp salad.

Per serving: Calories: 370; Total Fat: 30g; Saturated Fat: 4g; Cholesterol: 248mg; Sodium: 306mg; Carbohydrates: 2g; Fiber: 0g; Protein: 27g

Margherita Buddha Bowl

YIELD: 2 CUPS / PREP TIME: 15 MINUTES / COOK TIME: 25 MINUTES

GLUTEN FREE, NUT FREE

Enter a state of culinary bliss thanks to this flavorful Margherita Buddha Bowl. This hearty and vibrant vegetarian bowl serves up classic Italian flavors of fresh mozzarella, tomato, basil, balsamic vinegar, and olive oil amid healthy grains and veggies. Consider making the quinoa a day ahead to save time, and switch up the veggies if you have any leftovers.

¼ cup quinoa

½ cup unsalted vegetable broth

¼ cup fresh baby mozzarella balls (bocconcini balls) or ¼-inch-thick fresh mozzarella slices

¼ cup canned garbanzo beans (chickpeas), rinsed and drained

½ cup chopped plum tomatoes

¼ cup kalamata olives

¼ cup peeled and diced cucumbers

¼ cup chopped fresh basil

2 tablespoons balsamic vinegar

4 tablespoons extra-virgin olive oil

1. Rinse the quinoa in a fine-mesh strainer under cold water and drain. In a 1-quart saucepan, bring the quinoa and vegetable broth to a boil over medium heat. Boil for 1 minute. Reduce the heat to low and simmer, covered, for an 15 additional minutes. Remove the pan from the heat and let it stand, covered, for 5 minutes.

2. In a medium shallow bowl, arrange the Buddha Bowl by placing piles of quinoa, baby mozzarella balls, chickpeas, tomatoes, olives, and cucumbers side by side to form a colorful, circular display. Sprinkle with basil.

3. In a small bowl, whisk together the balsamic vinegar and olive oil. Drizzle over the Buddha Bowl.

Variation Tip: If quinoa is not your grain of choice, try cooked barley or white, brown, jasmine, basmati, or sticky rice instead.

Per serving: Calories: 831; Total Fat: 69g; Saturated Fat: 13g; Cholesterol: 30mg; Sodium: 607mg; Carbohydrates: 41g; Fiber: 5g; Protein: 15g

Mediterranean Tuna–Stuffed Tomatoes

YIELD: 2 STUFFED TOMATOES / PREP TIME: 15 MINUTES

DAIRY FREE, GLUTEN FREE, NUT FREE, QUICK MEAL

A great way to rejuvenate basic tuna, these lively stuffed tomatoes with a briny Mediterranean twist are easy to make, healthy, and irresistible. Use yellow or red tomatoes for this recipe. Yellow tomatoes offer higher amounts of B vitamins and minerals, while red ones offer abundant amounts of vitamin A and lycopene, a powerful antioxidant that helps protect against cell damage. Since yellow tomatoes are higher in sodium, be sure to taste before adding salt.

1 (2.5-ounce pouch) tuna or 1 (5-ounce) canned tuna in water, drained

1 tablespoon diced celery

1 teaspoon minced shallot or red onion

½ teaspoon diced capers

½ teaspoon lemon juice

1 tablespoon mayonnaise

⅛ teaspoon oregano

1 tablespoon sliced ripe black olives

2 medium vine-ripe tomatoes

1. Place the drained tuna in a small mixing bowl. Fold in the celery, shallot or onion, capers, lemon juice, mayonnaise, oregano, and olives until well combined.

2. Using a sharp paring knife, cut the tops off of the tomatoes, about ½ inch down from the stem end. Scoop out the pulp and seeds. Reserve the pulp to use in sauces, if desired. Turn the tomatoes over, cut-side down, and cut a thin slice from the bottom, to stand for stability. Turn tomatoes right-side up again, and spoon tuna salad into tomatoes. Serve alone, or with a small tossed salad.

Variation Tip: Mix up your tuna salad by adding chopped spinach, arugula, or watercress. Or mix up your vessel by stuffing a yellow pepper.

Per serving: Calories: 247; Total Fat: 12g; Saturated Fat: 2g; Cholesterol: 31mg; Sodium: 267mg; Carbohydrates: 11g; Fiber: 4g; Protein: 24g

Roasted Vegetable Quesadilla

YIELD: 1 QUESADILLA / PREP TIME: 10 MINUTES / COOK TIME: 35 MINUTES

GOOD FOR LEFTOVERS, NUT FREE

My Roasted Vegetable Quesadilla boasts healthy root vegetables like sweet potatoes and beets, but it doesn't just taste delicious; this lunch is also infused with vitamin A, potassium, magnesium, and a boost of fiber. As a time saver, consider cutting and roasting the veggies in advance. If lemon pepper is nowhere to be found, use lemon zest and freshly ground black pepper instead.

¼ cup red potatoes, skin on, cut into ¼-inch pieces

¼ cup sweet potatoes, peeled, cut into ¼-inch pieces

¼ cup raw red beets, peeled, cut into ¼-inch pieces

¼ cup chopped red onion

¼ cup baby carrots

1 tablespoon extra-virgin olive oil

1 tablespoon lemon pepper seasoning

Cooking spray

1 (10-inch) flour tortilla

⅓ cup shredded part-skim Cheddar cheese

1. Preheat oven to 375°F.
2. Place the red potatoes, sweet potatoes, beets, onion, carrots, olive oil, and lemon pepper seasoning in a resealable 1-quart plastic bag. Toss the vegetables to coat thoroughly. Spread the vegetables on a baking pan in a single, even layer. Bake for about 20 to 25 minutes, until vegetables are softened.
3. Spray a griddle or medium sauté pan with cooking spray over medium-low heat until it shimmers, about 1 minute. Place the tortilla on the griddle. Add the shredded cheese, covering leaving ½ inch of tortilla edge bare. Add the roasted vegetables to half of the tortilla, allowing space to fold the quesadilla closed. Fry the closed quesadilla until it is golden brown and crisp, about 5 minutes per side. If the tortilla isn't crisping, add a few drops of vegetable oil to the griddle surface and continue cooking.

Variation Tip: Chop any extra roasted vegetables in a food processor to make a purée to help thicken soups or sauces.

Per serving: Calories: 574; Total Fat: 33g; Saturated Fat: 12g; Cholesterol: 40mg; Sodium: 857mg; Carbohydrates: 54g; Fiber: 5g; Protein: 16g

Stuffed Pepper, Beef, and Rice Soup

YIELD: 2 CUPS / PREP TIME: 15 MINUTES / COOK TIME: 30 MINUTES

GLUTEN FREE, GOOD FOR LEFTOVERS, MAKE AHEAD, NUT FREE

This comforting taste of home uses a combination of vegetable broth and juices, and tomato sauce to incorporate nutritious layers of flavor. This soup pairs well with a tossed salad or your favorite steamed vegetable.

1 tablespoon vegetable oil

¼ pound lean ground beef (85 percent lean)

1 medium green bell pepper, cut into 1½-inch pieces

¼ cup diced yellow onion

¼ teaspoon kosher salt

⅛ teaspoon freshly ground black pepper

¼ cup unsalted vegetable stock

½ cup unsalted tomato sauce

¼ cup vegetable juice or tomato juice

½ teaspoon Worcestershire sauce

¼ teaspoon dried oregano

¼ teaspoon dried basil

½ cup cooked rice (such as white, brown, jasmine, or basmati)

Grated Parmesan cheese (optional)

1. Heat a small sauté pan over medium heat. Add the oil to the pan and heat until it shimmers, about 1 minute. Add the ground beef, bell pepper, onion, salt, and black pepper, cooking for about 10 minutes, or until the ground beef is thoroughly browned, and the vegetables are softened. Drain off any excess grease from the beef before adding to the soup broth.

2. In a 2-quart saucepan, heat the vegetable stock, tomato sauce, vegetable juice, Worcestershire sauce, oregano, and basil to a boil over medium heat. Boil for 1 minute, then reduce heat to low and simmer to blend flavors, about 5 minutes more.

3. Fold the ground beef mixture into the broth, stirring occasionally until thoroughly heated and the temperature reaches 165°F. Fold in the cooked rice and continue simmering over medium-low heat for an additional 5 minutes. Serve with grated Parmesan cheese if you like.

Per serving: Calories: 552; Total Fat: 32g; Saturated Fat: 8g; Cholesterol: 75mg; Sodium: 491mg; Carbohydrates: 42g; Fiber: 9g; Protein: 26g

Teriyaki Chicken Burger

YIELD: 1 SANDWICH / PREP TIME: 10 MINUTES / COOK TIME: 15 MINUTES

NUT FREE, QUICK MEAL

Teriyaki sauce traces its origin to Japanese immigrants in Hawaii. This homemade version sticks closely to the original, fusing pineapple juice with traditional soy, ginger, and rice vinegar to top a juicy chicken burger. To arrive at just the right level of burger juiciness, first brown the patty before finishing it in the oven. If you do not have an oven-safe skillet, transfer the burger to a baking sheet to finish cooking.

1 tablespoon vegetable oil

¼ pound ground chicken

⅛ teaspoon kosher salt

⅛ teaspoon freshly ground black pepper

2 tablespoons pineapple juice

1 teaspoon rice vinegar

1 teaspoon granulated sugar

1 teaspoon brown sugar

3 tablespoons soy sauce

½ teaspoon minced fresh ginger

2 tablespoons water

1 tablespoon cornstarch

1 hamburger bun or kaiser roll

1. Preheat oven to 350°F.

2. Heat a small oven-safe sauté pan over medium heat. Add the oil to the pan and heat until it shimmers, about 1 minute. Shape the ground chicken into a patty and season with salt and pepper. Fry the burger on both sides until evenly browned, about 2 minutes per side. Finish cooking the burger in the preheated oven, until it is cooked through and the internal temperature reaches 165°F, about 10 minutes more.

3. Turn the burner to medium heat. In a 1-quart saucepan, whisk together the pineapple juice, rice vinegar, granulated sugar, brown sugar, soy sauce, ginger, water, and cornstarch. Cook, whisking constantly until the sauce thickens, about 2 to 3 minutes.

4. Remove the chicken burger from the oven and place on the burger bun. Add the sauce to the cooked chicken burger.

Variation Tip: Grill slices of pineapple and red onion to top the burger. Just add a few drops of vegetable oil to the grill or griddle to keep them from sticking.

Per serving: Calories: 510; Total Fat: 25g; Saturated Fat: 4g; Cholesterol: 96mg; Sodium: 3,057mg; Carbohydrates: 44g; Fiber: 2g; Protein: 27g

Turkey Monte Cristo

YIELD: 1 SANDWICH / PREP TIME: 10 MINUTES / COOK TIME: 15 MINUTES

5 INGREDIENTS OR FEWER, NUT FREE, QUICK MEAL

The Monte Cristo is the American take on the French *croque monsieur*. I've modernized this recipe using all turkey rather than ham, and low-salt Swiss cheese to minimize sodium. I lightly batter one side of the bread to avoid the sandwich becoming too soggy. It's a good idea to fry the bread open-faced for about 10 minutes until it becomes browned and firm, like French toast.

Cooking spray

1 large egg

1 tablespoon reduced-fat (2-percent) milk

2 slices white bread

2 slices low-sodium Swiss cheese

4 ounces sliced deli turkey breast (about 4 slices)

1. Heat a griddle lightly sprayed with cooking spray over medium-low heat for about 1 minute.

2. In a shallow bowl, whisk together the egg and milk to form a batter. Dip one side of the bread in the egg mixture and place it on the hot griddle. Repeat with the other slice of bread. Add 1 slice of cheese on top of each slice of bread.

3. Place the turkey slices on the empty side of the griddle. Add cooking spray if necessary to avoid the turkey sticking to the griddle. Fry the turkey to thoroughly heat and lightly brown, 2 to 3 minutes. Place the hot turkey on both sides of the open sandwich. The hot turkey will help melt the cheese. Close the sandwich and transfer to a serving plate.

Variation Tip: For classic French toast appeal, add a few drops of vanilla extract and a sprinkle of cinnamon. Serve with syrup or powdered sugar if you like.

Per serving: Calories: 493; Total Fat: 19g; Saturated Fat: 10g; Cholesterol: 255mg; Sodium: 1,567mg; Carbohydrates: 32g; Fiber: 1g; Protein: 46g

Tuscan Bean Soup

YIELD: 2 CUPS / PREP TIME: 15 MINUTES / COOK TIME: 15 MINUTES

DAIRY FREE, GLUTEN FREE, NUT FREE, VEGAN

Characterized by simple food unadorned by heavy sauces, Tuscan cooking is rustic, humble, and pure in flavor and ingredients. My Tuscan Bean Soup recipe follows this tradition of simplicity, both in taste and technique. Simple though the ingredients may be, this soup is anything but boring. It boasts a hearty, pleasing texture and flavor from quickly mashed, high-protein cannellini beans. The beans make this lightly seasoned vegan soup a truly fortifying meatless choice.

1 tablespoon extra-virgin olive oil

½ cup thickly sliced carrots

¼ cup roughly chopped onion

½ cup roughly chopped celery

1 clove minced garlic

¼ teaspoon dried oregano

2 fresh thyme sprigs

⅛ teaspoon kosher salt

⅛ teaspoon freshly ground black pepper

2 cups unsalted vegetable stock

½ cup baby spinach

1 cup rinsed canned cannellini beans, divided

1. Heat olive oil in a 2-quart saucepan over medium heat for about 1 minute until glistening. Add the carrots, onion, celery, and garlic. Sauté the vegetables over medium-high heat for about 5 minutes until crisp-tender.

2. Reduce heat to low, add the oregano, thyme sprigs, salt, pepper, vegetable stock, and spinach. Simmer until warm, about 5 minutes.

3. In a small mixing bowl, place ¼ cup of beans. Mash the beans with a fork to keep them from getting too mushy. Set aside.

4. Add the remaining ¾ cup whole beans and the mashed beans to the soup pot. Gently stir to mix them into the soup. Increase the heat to medium-low and simmer until thoroughly heated; the internal temperature should reach 165°F. Remove the thyme sprigs. Serve.

Variation Tip: Add ½ cup of canned Italian-style diced tomatoes, navy beans, and kale, chard, or collard greens for a more robust taste. If using heartier greens, add them at the beginning of the cooking process.

Per serving: Calories: 403; Total Fat: 15g; Saturated Fat: 2g; Cholesterol: 0mg; Sodium: 175mg; Carbohydrates: 53g; Fiber: 17g; Protein: 17g

SUN-DRIED TOMATO
PESTO TORTELLINI, PAGE 68

CHAPTER FOUR

MEATLESS MAINS FOR ONE

Growing up, I was constantly instructed, "Eat your vegetables. You need them to grow!"—a statement all too often punctuated by the sad peas rolling all over my plate. In that era, vegetables seemed like a mere afterthought of a side dish, a necessary evil. Today, they take center stage in countless delicious and creative recipes. What's more, plant-based protein is easy to find in beans, tofu, tempeh, nuts, and grains! Though it was once a chore, downing those vegetables has become something to enjoy!

Buffalo Tofu Pasta Bake

YIELD: 2 CUPS / PREP TIME: 15 MINUTES / COOK TIME: 30 MINUTES

BAKE AND SERVE, GOOD FOR LEFTOVERS, MAKE AHEAD, NUT FREE

Proving that this classic and zesty sauce isn't just for chicken wings anymore, this hearty, filling, and comforting Buffalo Tofu Pasta Bake marries the tingling taste of the iconic sauce with cubes of firm tofu and tender noodles. To lend a satisfying crunch factor, toasted bread crumbs bring a touch of texture to the dish, contrasting nicely with the softer tofu and noodles. If you want to boost the vitamin content and add a bit more vegetable heft, consider adding chopped broccoli or carrots to the dish when you combine the buffalo sauce, tofu, and noodles, just before the casserole gets topped with panko and popped into the oven.

1 cup dry medium-wide noodles

Cooking spray

2 ounces extra firm tofu, sliced into 1-inch-thick slices and pressed (refer to Garlic Tofu Cobb Salad, page 42, for pressing directions)

⅛ teaspoon garlic powder

½ teaspoon kosher salt, divided

⅛ teaspoon freshly ground black pepper

3 tablespoons unsalted butter, divided

1 tablespoon hot sauce

¼ cup panko bread crumbs

1 teaspoon freshly chopped or dried parsley

1. Preheat oven to 350°F.
2. Cook the noodles according to package directions in salted water. Drain, then place in a small 1.5-quart casserole dish.
3. Heat a griddle, small sauté pan, or skillet lightly sprayed with cooking spray over medium-high heat until hot. Dust the tofu with garlic powder, ⅛ teaspoon salt, and pepper. Fry the tofu on the hot griddle until firm and thoroughly cooked, about 5 minutes per side, turning with tongs halfway through cooking. Cut the cooked tofu into ½-inch pieces and fold into the cooked noodles.
4. Heat 2 tablespoons butter in the microwave for 5-second intervals until completely melted. Add the hot sauce and stir until evenly combined. Pour over the tofu and noodles. Stir to coat evenly.
5. Heat a small sauté pan over medium-high heat for 1 minute. In a small mixing bowl, combine remaining 1 tablespoon butter, panko, ⅛ teaspoon salt, and parsley. Add to the pan. Sauté, stirring often, until the bread crumbs have browned and absorbed the butter, about 5 minutes. Sprinkle over the top of the casserole. Bake for about 10 minutes, or until thoroughly heated.

Variation Tip: Leftover Buffalo Tofu Pasta Bake can be made into a zesty pasta salad. Stir in chopped broccoli, cauliflower, or carrots. Whisk together 1 tablespoon apple cider vinegar with 2 tablespoons extra-virgin olive oil as a dressing.

Per serving: Calories: 530; Total Fat: 39g; Saturated Fat: 23g; Cholesterol: 124mg; Sodium: 664mg; Carbohydrates: 36g; Fiber: 3g; Protein: 12g

Fennel, Tomatoes, and Butter Beans

YIELD: 2 CUPS / PREP TIME: 10 MINUTES / COOK TIME: 15 MINUTES

GLUTEN FREE, NUT FREE, ONE POT, QUICK MEAL, VEGAN

This one-pan wonder combines fennel, tomatoes, and butter beans for a seriously hearty vegan meal. Fennel is an excellent source of fiber and adds a delicate, sweet anise flavor that complements the smooth butter beans and juicy tomatoes. Parsley brightens the dish and adds that fresh kick.

2 tablespoons unsalted vegan, nut free butter

1 bay leaf

1 large ripe tomato, sliced

½ cup sliced fennel

2 tablespoons gluten free flour

½ cup vegetable stock

⅛ teaspoon kosher salt

⅛ teaspoon ground pepper

1 cup canned butter beans, rinsed and drained

1 tablespoon chopped fresh parsley to garnish (optional)

1. Heat a medium sauté pan over medium heat for 1 minute. Melt the butter in the pan. Add the bay leaf, tomatoes, and fennel to the pan and sauté until soft, about 5 minutes.

2. In a small mixing bowl, whisk together the flour, stock, salt, and pepper. Reduce heat to low and stir the flour mixture into the tomato-fennel mixture and simmer until thickened, about 5 minutes.

3. Remove the bay leaf and gently fold the beans into the tomato-fennel sauce. Simmer on low heat until thoroughly heated, about 5 minutes. If desired, thin the sauce by stirring in additional vegetable stock, 1 tablespoon at a time, until the sauce reaches the desired consistency. Garnish with parsley, if desired.

Cooking Tip: Purchased vegetable stocks vary greatly both in intensity of flavor and salt content, and canned beans can have a high salt content, even after rinsing. The salt measurements in these recipes should serve as a guide.

Per serving: Calories: 429; Total Fat: 25g; Saturated Fat: 18g; Cholesterol: 60mg; Sodium: 742mg; Carbohydrates: 43g; Fiber: 9g; Protein: 11g

Garden Burgers

YIELD: 2 BURGERS / PREP TIME: 15 MINUTES / COOK TIME: 10 MINUTES

DAIRY FREE, GOOD FOR LEFTOVERS, NUT FREE, VEGAN

For this burger, through much trial and error, I settled upon a black bean base. I have found it most suited to the occasion because it is moist, firm, versatile, and most importantly, flavor-packed.

2 teaspoons vegetable oil

½ cup minced yellow onion

¼ cup diced roasted red peppers, drained

1 cup canned black beans, rinsed and drained

1 slice white bread, crust removed, cut into
½-inch pieces

¼ teaspoon kosher salt

½ teaspoon garlic powder

¼ cup all-purpose flour

Cooking spray

1. Heat a small sauté pan over medium heat. Add the oil to the pan and heat until it shimmers, about 1 minute. Sauté the onions and roasted red peppers until the onions begin to soften, about 4 to 5 minutes.

2. Place the beans in a medium mixing bowl. Mash the beans with a potato masher or fork until only a few lumps remain. Mix in the cooked onions and peppers, bread, salt, and garlic powder by hand. Add the flour, 1 tablespoon at a time, until the beans form a dough you can shape into burger patties with your hands. Form into 2 patties, about ½-inch thick.

3. Spray a griddle or small sauté pan with cooking spray. Fry the burgers over medium-low heat until brown on both sides and thoroughly heated through, about 4 to 5 minutes per side.

Solo Storage Tip: Freeze cooked patties for later use by layering burgers between wax paper and storing them in an airtight freezer bag. When you're ready to enjoy, just reheat the burgers in the oven at 350°F for 10 to 15 minutes, or in a microwave for 1 to 2 minutes until thoroughly heated.

Per serving: Calories: 542; Total Fat: 12g; Saturated Fat: 1g; Cholesterol: 0mg; Sodium: 360mg; Carbohydrates: 89g; Fiber: 18g; Protein: 22g

Garden Vegetable Pita Pizzas

YIELD: 1 SERVING / PREP TIME: 10 MINUTES / COOK TIME: 15 MINUTES

GOOD FOR LEFTOVERS, NUT FREE, ONE POT, QUICK MEAL

In my Garden Vegetable Pita Pizza, we dodge the dough hassle by using pita bread, which makes the perfect-size pizza for one. Adding to the ease, the recipe utilizes vegetables that cook in the same amount of time. Not feeling the tomato sauce? Make it a white pizza with olive oil and chopped garlic.

1 pita bread (white or wheat)

¼ cup canned pizza sauce

½ cup shredded mozzarella cheese

½ chopped plum tomato

1 tablespoon chopped green bell pepper

1 tablespoon chopped red onion

¼ cup chopped broccoli

¼ cup chopped zucchini

1. Preheat oven to 400°F.
2. Place the pita bread on a baking sheet. Add the sauce and shredded cheese. Sprinkle the tomato, pepper, onion, broccoli, and zucchini evenly over the cheese.
3. Bake for about 15 minutes, until vegetables are softened and cheese has thoroughly melted. Cut in quarters before serving.

Solo Storage Tip: Make individual pita pizzas with a variety of toppings and freeze to enjoy later. Place a piece of wax paper or parchment between pizzas for easy separation. To reheat, pop them into a 400°F oven for 5 to 10 minutes, checking often so the pitas won't burn.

Per serving: Calories: 386; Total Fat: 11g; Saturated Fat: 7g; Cholesterol: 30mg; Sodium: 725mg; Carbohydrates: 50g; Fiber: 5g; Protein: 22g

Greek Stuffed Zucchini Boats

YIELD: 2 BOATS, 1 SERVING / PREP TIME: 10 MINUTES / COOK TIME: 20 MINUTES

BAKE AND SERVE, GLUTEN FREE, GOOD FOR LEFTOVERS, QUICK MEAL

Picture yourself sailing the Mediterranean when you enjoy these Greek Stuffed Zucchini Boats. Simply combine pungent feta cheese and robust garlic with tomato, onion, and peppers to fill scooped-out zucchini halves. Finish with a drizzle of cucumber tzatziki sauce. Be mindful to not overbake so the zucchini will retain its shape, yet be perfectly cooked and not mushy.

1 medium-size zucchini, halved

½ diced plum tomato (about 2 tablespoons)

1 tablespoon minced red bell pepper

1 tablespoon minced red onion

1 tablespoon crumbled feta cheese

¼ cup diced cucumber

½ cup plain low-fat yogurt

1 teaspoon lemon juice

½ teaspoon chopped fresh dill

⅛ teaspoon minced garlic

1/16 teaspoon kosher salt

1/16 teaspoon freshly ground black pepper

1. Preheat oven to 350°F.

2. Scoop out the insides of the zucchini halves with a teaspoon, being careful to leave the outer walls intact, with about ¼-inch outer thickness remaining. Fill the zucchini boats with the tomatoes, bell peppers, onion, and feta.

3. Place the filled zucchini boats on a baking sheet on the center rack of the oven. Bake for 15 to 20 minutes until softened but not mushy.

4. Place cucumber pieces on paper towels and pat away excess moisture. In a small mixing bowl, whisk together the yogurt, lemon juice, dill, garlic, salt, and pepper. Fold the cucumber pieces into the sauce. Drizzle tzatziki sauce over the baked zucchini boats.

Variation Tip: If you have cooked zucchini boats left over, they can be chopped and added to Greek or Caesar salads.

Per serving: Calories: 201; Total Fat: 4g; Saturated Fat: 3g; Cholesterol: 16mg; Sodium: 346mg; Carbohydrates: 29g; Fiber: 5g; Protein: 13g

Mushroom Stroganoff

YIELD: 2 CUPS / PREP TIME: 10 MINUTES / COOK TIME: 25 MINUTES

BAKE AND SERVE, GOOD FOR LEFTOVERS, NUT FREE

This vegetarian variation on the hearty Russian classic works so well because portobello mushrooms have a meaty texture. To make this a vegan meal, omit the sour cream and double the gravy ingredients. Either way, the mushrooms are the standouts of this luscious dish.

1 cup dry medium-size noodles

2 tablespoons vegetable oil, divided

½ cup sliced portobello mushrooms

1 tablespoon all-purpose flour

¾ cup vegetable broth, divided

2 fresh thyme sprigs or ¼ teaspoon dried thyme

1 tablespoon low-fat sour cream

1 tablespoon chopped fresh parsley

1. Cook noodles according to package directions. Drain.

2. Heat a small sauté pan over medium heat for 1 minute. Add 1 tablespoon oil and heat until it shimmers, about 1 minute. Sauté the mushrooms in the pan for 5 minutes, or until soft and lightly browned. Transfer the mushrooms to a plate.

3. Return the pan to medium heat and add remaining 1 tablespoon oil and flour, which will thicken the gravy. Sauté the oil and flour together, occasionally stirring with a heat-resistant spatula until the mixture is golden in color and begins to form small bubbles, about 1 minute. Remove from heat.

4. Stir in ¼ cup vegetable broth to form a roux, which will resemble a thick paste. Return the pan to the stovetop and reduce heat to low. Stir in the remaining ½ cup broth and add the thyme. Return the mushrooms to the pan. Add the sour cream and keep stirring until it is evenly combined. Add the noodles and stir to coat. Cook until thoroughly heated, an additional 2 minutes. If using thyme sprigs, remove them from the pan. Sprinkle with parsley.

Per serving: Calories: 484; Total Fat: 33g; Saturated Fat: 5g; Cholesterol: 38mg; Sodium: 592mg; Carbohydrates: 37g; Fiber: 2g; Protein: 12g

Ratatouille

YIELD: 2 CUPS / PREP TIME: 15 MINUTES / COOK TIME: 30 MINUTES

DAIRY FREE, GLUTEN FREE, NUT FREE, ONE POT, VEGAN

In French, *Ratatouille* means to "stir it up" and that is just what we do with this entrée. The flavors in this recipe are layered and nuanced. Mop up your plate with good-quality gluten free crusty bread!

2 tablespoons extra-virgin olive oil

¼ cup diced yellow onion

⅛ teaspoon kosher salt

¼ teaspoon crushed red pepper flakes

¼ cup diced green bell peppers

¼ cup diced plum tomatoes

½ cup tomato juice

½ teaspoon minced garlic

¼ teaspoon dried oregano

2 fresh thyme sprigs or ¼ teaspoon dried thyme

¼ cup diced peeled eggplant

¼ cup diced yellow squash

¼ cup diced zucchini

1 tablespoon chopped fresh basil

1. Heat a medium sauté pan over medium heat for about 1 minute. Drizzle the oil into the pan and heat until it shimmers about 1 minute.

2. Add the onions, salt, red pepper flakes, and bell peppers. Cook over medium heat, stirring occasionally until onions and peppers are crisp-tender, about 2 minutes.

3. Stir in the tomatoes, tomato juice, garlic, oregano, and thyme. Simmer an additional 5 minutes to break down the tomatoes into a soft pulp.

4. Reduce heat to low and fold in the eggplant, squash, zucchini, and basil. Simmer another 10 minutes, or until the sauce has thickened. If using thyme sprigs, remove them from the pan. Serve ratatouille with crusty bread for dipping, if you like.

Cooking Tip: Salting eggplant before cooking draws out excess moisture for even cooking. Place eggplant pieces in a single layer on paper towels. Sprinkle enough kosher salt to cover the pieces. Top eggplant with another layer of paper towels. Gently press out excess moisture.

Per serving: Calories: 308; Total Fat: 29g; Saturated Fat: 4g; Cholesterol: 0mg; Sodium: 417mg; Carbohydrates: 16g; Fiber: 4g; Protein: 3g

Roasted Vegetable Lasagna

YIELD: 1 SERVING / PREP TIME: 15 MINUTES / COOK TIME: 1 HOUR 15 MINUTES

BAKE AND SERVE, MAKE AHEAD, NUT FREE

This comforting Roasted Vegetable Lasagna offers a vegetarian version of a classic dish. You can cut the prep time by roasting the vegetables the day before prepping the lasagna, and using oven-ready lasagna noodles that require no boiling.

½ cup peeled sweet potatoes, cut into ¼-inch pieces

¼ cup chopped broccoli

¼ cup chopped red onion

¼ cup baby carrots

¼ cup diced zucchini

1 tablespoon extra-virgin olive oil

¼ teaspoon oregano

½ teaspoon dried thyme

¼ teaspoon rosemary

¼ teaspoon kosher salt

1 cup spaghetti sauce, divided

3 oven-ready lasagna noodles or cooked regular lasagna noodles

½ cup part-skim ricotta cheese, divided

½ cup part-skim shredded mozzarella, divided

1. Preheat oven to 375°F.
2. In a 1-quart resealable plastic bag, combine the sweet potatoes, broccoli, onion, carrots, zucchini, oil, oregano, thyme, rosemary, and salt. Shake the bag to coat the vegetables with oil and herbs. Place the vegetables in a single layer on a baking sheet. Bake for 20 to 25 minutes or until vegetables are soft but not mushy.
3. Layer ¼ cup spaghetti sauce in the bottom of a 1½-quart baking dish. Top with 1 lasagna noodle. Spread ¼ cup ricotta cheese over the noodle. Sprinkle 2 tablespoons shredded mozzarella over the ricotta. Spoon half the roasted vegetables and another ¼ cup of sauce over the cheese. Top with the second noodle. Spread the remaining ¼ cup ricotta and sprinkle 2 tablespoons mozzarella over the noodle. Pour on ¼ cup sauce and the rest of the vegetables. Top with the remaining noodle, ¼ cup sauce, and mozzarella.
4. Cover with foil and bake for 50 to 60 minutes, or until internal temperature reaches 165°F and cheese is melted.

Per serving: Calories: 787; Total Fat: 37g; Saturated Fat: 14g; Cholesterol: 98mg; Sodium: 1,020mg; Carbohydrates: 76g; Fiber: 8g; Protein: 44g

Sautéed Cabbage and Noodles

YIELD: 2 CUPS / PREP TIME: 10 MINUTES / COOK TIME: 30 MINUTES

GOOD FOR LEFTOVERS, MAKE AHEAD, NUT FREE

Sautéed Cabbage and Noodles is a Pennsylvania favorite that's made several different ways, all depending upon regional preference. Where I grew up, the cabbage was fried with bacon and loads of butter and onions. Others used red cabbage braised in broth. I chose to include a vegetarian version that's still deeply flavorful, nourishing, and indulgent. To vary the texture and add substance, substitute collard greens, fennel, or kohlrabi for the cabbage. Leftover raw cabbage can be used in a slaw or stir-fry.

2 tablespoons unsalted butter

2 tablespoons extra-virgin olive oil

¼ head of green cabbage, thinly sliced (about 2 cups)

¼ cup thinly sliced yellow onion

¼ teaspoon kosher salt

⅛ teaspoon freshly ground black pepper

1 cup medium-size noodles

1. Heat a medium sauté pan over medium heat for about 1 minute. Melt the butter with the olive oil.

2. Add the cabbage, onions, salt, and pepper to the pan and stir to combine. Cover the pan and reduce to a simmer over low to medium heat, turning occasionally to brown but not burn the cabbage and onions, about 25 to 30 minutes.

3. Cook the noodles according to the package directions. Drain.

4. Fold the cooked noodles into the finished cabbage and onions and stir to coat.

Variation Tip: Leftover Sautéed Cabbage and Noodles can be integrated into any vegetable soup recipe. Just add broth and your favorite additional vegetables to create a new lunch for your meal plan.

Per serving: Calories: 643; Total Fat: 52g; Saturated Fat: 21g; Cholesterol: 92mg; Sodium: 191mg; Carbohydrates: 40g; Fiber: 6g; Protein: 8g

Spaghetti Squash with Stewed Tomatoes

YIELD: 2 CUPS / PREP TIME: 10 MINUTES / COOK TIME: 45 MINUTES

BAKE AND SERVE, GOOD FOR LEFTOVERS, MAKE AHEAD

You may be surprised to see what a great, healthy substitute spaghetti squash makes for pasta. With their similar textures, it's hard to tell the difference once you add sauce and cheese. The secret to good spaghetti squash is not to overcook, so check often while baking or boiling to prevent this.

½ cut medium spaghetti squash, seeds and pulp removed

1 cup water

1 tablespoon extra-virgin olive oil

½ cup sliced onions

2 cups mixed bell pepper slices

1 cup canned stewed tomatoes

1 teaspoon dried oregano

½ teaspoon kosher salt

⅛ teaspoon freshly ground black pepper

½ cup freshly shredded Parmesan cheese

1 cup part-skim shredded mozzarella cheese

1. Preheat oven to 350°F.
2. Place the squash cut-side down in a shallow baking dish. Add 1 cup water. Bake until the skin indents when gently pressed with your finger, about 20 minutes. While the spaghetti squash cooks, prepare the vegetables.
3. Heat a small sauté pan over medium heat. Add the olive oil to the pan and heat until it shimmers. Sauté the onions, bell peppers, and tomatoes until the vegetables are tender, about 5 minutes. Sprinkle the vegetables with the oregano, salt, and black pepper.
4. Using tongs, transfer the cooked spaghetti squash from the oven to a plate and cool for 5 minutes. Shred the squash onto a plate with a fork by drawing the fork tines along the squash flesh to create long yellow strands.
5. Add the shredded squash to the cooked vegetables. Place the mixture in a shallow baking dish. Top with cheeses. Bake for 20 minutes, or until cheeses melt and are golden brown.

Variation Tip: For a delicious alternative, try 1 cup cooked shredded spaghetti squash sautéed over low heat in a small sauté pan or skillet with ¼ cup baby spinach, 1 tablespoon pine nuts, ½ teaspoon minced garlic, ¼ teaspoon balsamic vinegar, and 1 teaspoon olive oil.

Per serving: Calories: 764; Total Fat: 46g; Saturated Fat: 22g; Cholesterol: 112mg; Sodium: 1,565mg; Carbohydrates: 45g; Fiber: 6g; Protein: 50g

Spicy Black-Eyed Peas and Rice

YIELD: 2 CUPS / PREP TIME: 10 MINUTES / COOK TIME: 20 MINUTES

DAIRY FREE, NUT FREE, QUICK MEAL, VEGAN

In this hearty and lively recipe, tender black-eyed peas and tomatoes soak up just the right amount of kick from jalapeños, garlic, chili powder, and a splash of hot sauce. Serve it with something to calm the zingy heat, perhaps a small salad or other favorite vegetable. For a heart-healthy option, try quinoa instead of rice.

1 cup canned black-eyed peas, rinsed and drained

1 cup diced canned tomatoes, with juices

½ diced jalapeño, seeded and membrane removed

½ teaspoon minced garlic

½ teaspoon chili powder

¼ teaspoon hot sauce

½ cup basmati or long-grain white rice

1 cup vegetable broth

1. Heat a 2-quart saucepan over medium heat. Add the black-eyed peas, tomatoes, jalapeño, garlic, chili powder, and hot sauce. Reduce heat to medium-low and cook for about 5 minutes to blend the flavors, stirring occasionally. Reduce heat to low to keep warm while the rice cooks.

2. In a 1-quart saucepan, heat the rice and vegetable broth to a boil over medium heat. When the broth begins to boil, reduce heat to low and cover. Cook for 15 minutes, or until rice has absorbed liquid and is tender. Pour the black-eyed pea mixture over the rice. Serve.

Substitution Tip: Easily dial down the heat in this dish by substituting smoked paprika for the chili powder and replacing the jalapeño with roasted poblano peppers.

Per serving: Calories: 507; Total Fat: 4g; Saturated Fat: 1g; Cholesterol: 10mg; Sodium: 747mg; Carbohydrates: 99g; Fiber: 8g; Protein: 19g

Sun-Dried Tomato Pesto Tortellini

YIELD: 2 CUPS / PREP TIME: 10 MINUTES / COOK TIME: 15 MINUTES

GOOD FOR LEFTOVERS, NUT FREE, QUICK MEAL

Pesto is one of my favorite sauces for so many reasons: It's easy to make, and the smell of fresh basil fills the house with its wonderful scent. When making pesto at home, you can customize it to your own tastes by adding or lessening garlic, olive oil, and cheese. This recipe brings a tantalizing new texture with the addition of sun-dried tomato.

½ cup sun-dried tomatoes, packed in oil

½ cup fresh basil

1 garlic clove

¼ cup grated Parmesan cheese

2 tablespoons extra-virgin olive oil

⅛ teaspoon kosher salt (optional)

1 teaspoon salt

2 cups frozen cheese tortellini

1. Grind the sun-dried tomatoes, basil, and garlic in a food processor into about ¼-inch size pieces. Add the cheese to the mixture and grind it into a paste.
2. Drizzle in 2 tablespoons olive oil gradually with the food processor running. Taste. Add kosher salt, if desired.
3. In a 3-quart saucepan, bring 2 quarts of salted water to a boil over high heat.
4. Add the frozen tortellini to the boiling water. Reduce the heat to medium. Boil the tortellini gently for 3 to 5 minutes until the pasta floats. Drain the tortellini, reserving about ½ cup of the pasta water.
5. Plate the pasta and toss with the pesto. If necessary, thin the pesto with a bit of reserved pasta water.

Solo Storage Tip: Sun-Dried Tomato Pesto can keep in a freezer bag in the refrigerator for 3 days, or freeze for up to 3 months. Thaw out the pesto while still in the bag. For a protein boost, add cooked chicken or shrimp to thawed bag. Reseal the bag and toss to coat.

Per serving: Calories: 637; Total Fat: 40g; Saturated Fat: 11g; Cholesterol: 50mg; Sodium: 937mg; Carbohydrates: 52g; Fiber: 5g; Protein: 24g

Sweet Potato and Lentil Turnovers

YIELD: 2 TURNOVERS / PREP TIME: 15 MINUTES / COOK TIME: 25 MINUTES

DAIRY FREE, GOOD FOR LEFTOVERS

The sweet potatoes packing these turnovers are high in vitamins A and C, while the lentils bring protein and a pleasantly contrasting bite. To avoid your turnovers going soggy, serve them immediately after cooking. Bake the remaining biscuits and freeze to serve later.

1 tablespoon vegetable oil

¼ cup chopped sweet potatoes

1 tablespoon diced onion

1 minced garlic clove

½ cup vegetable broth

1 teaspoon cornstarch

¼ cup cooked lentils

½ teaspoon Worcestershire sauce

2 tablespoons frozen diced carrot and pea blend, thawed

1 large egg

2 teaspoons water

¼ cup flour

1 (4.5-ounce) tube biscuit dough (large biscuit size)

1. Preheat oven to 400°F.

2. Heat a 2-quart saucepan over medium heat for 1 minute. Add the oil to the pan and heat until it shimmers, about 1 minute. Add the sweet potatoes, onion, and garlic. Sauté the vegetables, stirring occasionally, until the sweet potatoes form a light crust and onions are translucent, about 5 minutes.

3. In a small mixing bowl, whisk together the vegetable broth and cornstarch. Pour the broth mixture into a 1-quart saucepan and cook over medium-low heat, stirring occasionally to thicken, about 2 minutes. Stir in the cooked lentils and Worcestershire.

4. Add the lentils into the sweet potato mixture. Stir in the carrots and peas.

5. In a small mixing bowl, whisk together the egg and water.

6. Sprinkle a cutting board or smooth surface with flour. Roll out 2 biscuits into 7-inch rounds.

7. Scoop the filling onto the center of the dough dividing it evenly between 2 dough rounds. Brush the edge of the dough with egg wash halfway around to the middle. Pull the dry side of the dough over the filling to meet the wet edge. Using a fork, gently crimp the folded edge to seal each turnover. Using the fork tines, puncture the top of each turnover 3 or 4 times to allow steam to vent during baking.

CONTINUED ▸

8. Brush each turnover with egg wash and arrange them on a baking sheet 4 inches apart. Bake for 15 minutes, or until they are golden brown. Transfer to a plate and allow to cool for 3 to 4 minutes before serving.

Cooking Tip: To cook lentils, rinse them first to remove any debris. As a guideline, use 1 cup liquid for every ⅓ cup lentils. Bring water and lentils to a boil over medium-high heat in a 2-quart saucepan. Cover and reduce heat to low and simmer for about 15 to 20 minutes for whole lentils, 5 to 7 minutes for split peas and other split lentils. Salting after cooking helps lentils remain tender.

Per serving: Calories: 796; Total Fat: 35g; Saturated Fat: 10g; Cholesterol: 186mg; Sodium: 1,287mg; Carbohydrates: 94g; Fiber: 8g; Protein: 25g

Thai-Style Tempeh Stuffed Mushrooms

YIELD: 2 STUFFED MUSHROOMS / PREP TIME: 15 MINUTES / COOK TIME: 50 MINUTES / MARINATING TIME: 30 MINUTES

BAKE AND SERVE, MAKE AHEAD, VEGAN

Tempeh blends well with the classic Thai-influenced flavors in this recipe. The combination of sour, hot, bitter, and sweet creates a unique vegetarian dinner for one. To make the mushrooms softer, I recommend prebaking them before stuffing.

4 ounces tempeh, cut into ¼-inch pieces

1 tablespoon soy sauce

1 teaspoon sesame oil

1 teaspoon rice vinegar

½ teaspoon lime juice

2 tablespoons vegetable oil, divided

½ teaspoon minced garlic

1 teaspoon thinly sliced fresh ginger

1 teaspoon red curry paste

1 cup coconut milk

2 medium portobello mushrooms, stems and gills removed

1. Place tempeh, soy sauce, sesame oil, rice vinegar, and lime juice in a resealable bag in the refrigerator to marinate for 30 minutes before cooking.

2. Preheat oven to 350°F.

3. Heat a medium sauté pan over medium heat for about 1 minute. Add 1 tablespoon vegetable oil and heat until it shimmers, about 1 minute. Add the tempeh and fry about 3 minutes over medium heat, stirring constantly until golden brown.

4. In a small mixing bowl, whisk together garlic, ginger, curry paste, and coconut milk. Pour the sauce over the tempeh. Cook over medium heat until the sauce thickens, stirring occasionally, about 15 minutes.

5. Lightly coat the mushrooms with the remaining 1 tablespoon vegetable oil, then place them in a small baking dish. Bake for 25 minutes, or until mushrooms are softened but not mushy. Spoon the curried tempeh into the mushrooms. Bake them for an additional 10 to 15 minutes, or until thoroughly heated.

Per serving: Calories: 1,149; Total Fat: 104g; Saturated Fat: 58g; Cholesterol: 8mg; Sodium: 1,220mg; Carbohydrates: 39g; Fiber: 8g; Protein: 32g

Zoodles with Rustic Tomato Sauce

YIELD: 2 CUPS / PREP TIME: 15 MINUTES / COOK TIME: 20 MINUTES

GLUTEN FREE, NUT FREE, VEGAN

Zoodles, a colloquial name for zucchini noodles, headline this recipe and taste great with butter or a fresh tomato sauce. If you can't find already-spiraled zucchini, try thinly slicing zucchini to create ribbons.

1 plum tomato, chopped, seeds removed

2 tablespoons orange juice

2 tablespoons brown sugar

½ teaspoon cider vinegar

½ teaspoon fresh thyme leaves, or ¼ teaspoon dried thyme

2 cups home-cut or purchased zucchini noodles

1. Heat a 1-quart saucepan over medium heat for 1 minute. Add the tomatoes, orange juice, brown sugar, cider vinegar, and thyme and bring to a boil over medium heat. Boil for 1 minute, stirring occasionally.

2. Reduce heat to simmer. Cook until the tomatoes are soft, about 10 minutes, then mash tomatoes using a fork. The sauce will thicken slightly as it reduces.

3. In a 2-quart saucepan, bring 1.5 quarts of water to a boil. Reduce heat to medium. Add zoodles and gently cook, about 3 to 5 minutes, until just tender but not mushy. Drain. Fold sauce into the cooked noodles.

Variation Tip: Zucchini noodles taste best with light sauces like garlic oil or brown butter. Noodles made from the squash family can take a coating of any tomato-based sauce or pesto without breaking. Sweet potato noodles are a bit heartier and can be oven roasted as a side dish.

Per serving: Calories: 204; Total Fat: 1g; Saturated Fat: 0g; Cholesterol: 0mg; Sodium: 75mg; Carbohydrates: 46g; Fiber: 9g; Protein: 9g

COD WITH PICO DE GALLO, PAGE 80

CHAPTER FIVE

ONE IF BY SEA
(SOLO SEAFOOD RECIPES)

Years ago, I'd trek with my boss to South Philadelphia's lively, chaotic wholesale fish market. There, vendors lined the street with iced-down carts, selling everything from New England shrimp and crabs to whole fish and fillets like cod and flounder. I can't resist a satisfying dish made with fresh fish, shellfish, or inventively prepared canned fish. With a plethora of options for seafood today, solo cooks have so many choices to create simple, healthy, and satisfying fish meals with little muss or fuss.

Baked Fish Fillet

YIELD: 1 FILLET (3-OUNCE SERVING) / PREP TIME: 15 MINUTES / COOK TIME: 12 MINUTES

BAKE AND SERVE, DAIRY FREE, ONE POT, QUICK MEAL

With just a few adjustments, you can change the flavors of this versatile fish from classic bread crumbs to tingling Cajun spice. Keep your eye out for overcooking. At around 10 minutes, make a small cut at the thickest part of the fish. It should be flaky but opaque.

1 teaspoon vegetable oil

⅓ cup all-purpose flour

⅛ teaspoon salt

⅛ teaspoon freshly ground black pepper

1 large egg

½ cup plain bread crumbs

½ teaspoon dried parsley flakes

½ teaspoon seafood seasoning, store bought or homemade (see tip)

1 (3-ounce) cod fillet

1. Preheat oven to 400°F.
2. Lightly brush a baking sheet with oil.
3. Assemble a dredge station: Stir to mix the flour, salt, and pepper on one plate. In a small mixing bowl, lightly beat the egg. On a second plate, whisk together bread crumbs, parsley, and seafood seasoning.
4. Pat the cod dry with a paper towel. Dredge the cod using tongs, first in seasoned flour, shaking off excess flour. Dip the floured cod into the beaten egg, then place it on the bread-crumb plate. Using your hands, coat the cod with the seasoned crumbs and place the fish onto the baking sheet. Discard unused dredging ingredients.
5. Bake the cod for 10 to 12 minutes, flipping midway through when crumbs start browning. Bake until the fish is opaque, crumbs are lightly browned, and internal temperature reaches 145°F. Fish should flake easily with a fork.

Cooking Tip: Make seafood seasoning by whisking together 3 tablespoons kosher salt, 2 tablespoons ground celery seed, 1½ teaspoons dry mustard powder, 1½ teaspoons paprika, ¾ teaspoon freshly ground black pepper, ¾ teaspoon ground bay leaves, ¼ teaspoon ground ginger, ¼ teaspoon allspice, ¼ teaspoon cardamom, and ¼ teaspoon ground cinnamon. Store seasoning mix in a resealable plastic bag or airtight container for up to 3 months.

Per serving: Calories: 474; Total Fat: 12g; Saturated Fat: 2g; Cholesterol: 186mg; Sodium: 674mg; Carbohydrates: 58g; Fiber: 3g; Protein: 29g

Baked Salmon Noodle Casserole

YIELD: 2 CUPS / PREP TIME: 20 MINUTES / COOK TIME: 45 MINUTES

BAKE AND SERVE, MAKE AHEAD, NUT FREE

The delicate white sauce in this recipe reminds me of my mom's tuna casserole. Shake up the flavor profile by swapping in your favorite shredded cheese, perhaps Cheddar instead of Parmesan.

1 (4-ounce) salmon fillet, skin removed

½ teaspoon kosher salt, divided

½ teaspoon freshly ground black pepper, divided

2 teaspoons vegetable oil, divided

½ cup dry penne pasta

1 tablespoon cornstarch

1 cup reduced-fat (2-percent) milk

½ teaspoon dry mustard

2 tablespoons unsalted butter, divided

¼ cup grated Parmesan cheese, divided

2 tablespoons plain panko bread crumbs

1 tablespoon freshly chopped parsley

1. Preheat oven to 450°F.

2. Sprinkle the salmon with ¼ teaspoon salt and ¼ teaspoon pepper. Drizzle 1 teaspoon oil into a small baking dish. Drizzle the top of the salmon with the remaining 1 teaspoon oil and place in the baking dish. Bake the salmon for 10 minutes or until the salmon is opaque and easily flakes. Using an oven-safe spatula or fish spatula, transfer the fish to a plate. Cool slightly for 2 minutes, then flake the salmon. Reduce oven temperature to 350°F.

3. Cook the pasta according to package directions. Drain.

4. In a small mixing bowl, whisk the cornstarch in cold milk. In a 1-quart saucepan, heat the milk mixture with the mustard, remaining ¼ teaspoon salt, remaining ¼ teaspoon pepper, and 1 tablespoon butter over medium-low heat. Cook over medium-low heat, whisking constantly for about 5 to 6 minutes, until the butter melts and the sauce thickens. Remove the pan from the heat and stir in 2 tablespoons Parmesan cheese.

5. Heat a small sauté pan over medium heat for about 1 minute. Melt remaining 1 tablespoon butter in the pan. Stir the bread crumbs and remaining 2 tablespoons Parmesan cheese into the butter and cook, stirring occasionally for about 5 minutes until bread crumbs absorb the butter and turn golden brown.

CONTINUED ▸

Baked Salmon Noodle Casserole CONTINUED

6. In a medium mixing bowl, fold the cooked pasta, flaked salmon, and sauce together. Spread the casserole into a 2-quart baking dish. Sprinkle with prepared bread crumbs. Bake uncovered, for 15 minutes, or until the sauce thickens, the top of the casserole browns, and the internal temperature reaches 145°F. Garnish with additional parsley flakes.

Cooking Tip: To save time, make the salmon and noodles a day ahead. Combine flaked salmon and pasta in an airtight plastic bag, then refrigerate until ready to use.

Per serving: Calories: 1,015; Total Fat: 63g; Saturated Fat: 27g; Cholesterol: 163mg; Sodium: 683mg; Carbohydrates: 70g; Fiber: 4g; Protein: 47g

Clams Scampi

YIELD: 2 CUPS / PREP TIME: 20 MINUTES / COOK TIME: 15 MINUTES

NUT FREE, QUICK MEAL

In this straight-from-the-sea recipe, clams add a welcome briny flavor to garlicky, lemony, and buttery scampi. Be sure to buy fresh littleneck or cherrystone clams that are tightly closed. Store the clams in the refrigerator on a bowl of ice until ready to use.

1 tablespoon salt

6 fresh littleneck or cherrystone clams, tightly closed

4 tablespoons unsalted butter

1 tablespoon extra-virgin olive oil

1 tablespoon minced shallot

1 minced garlic clove

½ cup bottled clam juice

¼ cup white wine (Pinot Grigio or Chardonnay)

1 teaspoon lemon juice

⅛ teaspoon hot sauce

1 tablespoon fresh chopped parsley

¼ cup grated Parmesan cheese

2 ounces dry thin spaghetti (about ¼ of an 8-ounce box)

1. In a 2-quart bowl, whisk salt into 1 quart cold water. Soak the clams for about 10 minutes to loosen any outside dirt. The cold saltwater may stimulate the clams to open slightly. (That's okay as long as they close again when tapped.) Gently scrub shells with a clean cloth or vegetable brush to remove loosened sand and dirt.

2. Fill a 3-quart saucepan with 2 cups cold water. Heat on high until the water starts to boil. Use tongs to lower the clams into the boiling water. Cover with a lid and steam the clams for 3 to 4 minutes, or until the clams open fully. Transfer the opened clams in shells to a plate using tongs. Discard any unopened clams.

3. Heat a medium sauté pan over medium heat for 1 minute. Melt the butter in the pan. Add the olive oil, shallots, and garlic. Cook the shallots and garlic, stirring occasionally, until translucent, about 2 minutes.

4. Whisk in the clam juice, wine, and lemon juice. Reduce heat to low and simmer for 5 minutes, stirring often, until the sauce reduces by a third. Remove from the heat. Stir in the hot sauce, parsley, and Parmesan cheese.

5. Prepare pasta according to package directions. Drain. Transfer the cooked pasta to a dinner plate using tongs.

6. Using tongs, top pasta with clams in shells, then ladle sauce over pasta and clams.

Per serving: Calories: 949; Total Fat: 66g; Saturated Fat: 38g; Cholesterol: 170mg; Sodium: 1,136mg; Carbohydrates: 50g; Fiber: 3g; Protein: 36g

Cod with Pico de Gallo

YIELD: 1 SERVING / PREP TIME: 15 MINUTES / COOK TIME: 20 MINUTES

DAIRY FREE, GLUTEN FREE, GOOD FOR LEFTOVERS, NUT FREE, ONE POT

Pico de gallo, also known as *salsa fresca* or *salsa cruda*, makes a flavorful, fresh topping for many Mexican-inspired dishes. Culinary lore has it that pico de gallo was inspired by the red, white, and green Mexican flag, and flaky cod benefits from this juicy mix. Kept in the refrigerator, pico de gallo will stay fresh for up to four days and time only intensifies its vibrant flavor. Remove the jalapeño membrane and seeds before mincing to control the heat.

2 teaspoons vegetable oil

4 ounces cod

⅛ teaspoon kosher salt

1/16 teaspoon freshly ground black pepper

½ cup chopped fresh plum tomatoes

¼ cup chopped fresh green bell peppers

2 tablespoons chopped red onion

½ teaspoon minced fresh jalapeño pepper

½ teaspoon chopped fresh cilantro

Juice of ½ lime (about 1 tablespoon)

1. Preheat the oven to 400°F.
2. Drizzle the oil into a shallow ½-quart baking dish. Season the cod with a sprinkle of salt and ground pepper. Bake for 15 to 20 minutes, or until the fish turns opaque and easily flakes. When finished cooking, the interior of the fish should reach 145°F using a digital thermometer. Set fish aside on a separate plate.
3. In a small mixing bowl, stir together the tomatoes, bell peppers, onions, jalapeño, cilantro, lime juice, and remaining salt. Spoon the pico de gallo over the cod.

Variation Tip: Use extra Cod with Pico de Gallo for fish tacos. To shake up the fish choice, this recipe also works beautifully with catfish.

Per serving: Calories: 209; Total Fat: 10g; Saturated Fat: 1g; Cholesterol: 40mg; Sodium: 161mg; Carbohydrates: 10g; Fiber: 5g; Protein: 21g

Easy Fish and Chips

YIELD: 1 SERVING / PREP TIME: 10 MINUTES / COOK TIME: 25 MINUTES

DAIRY FREE, ONE POT

Pretend you're in an authentic British pub while in the comfort of your home with this recipe, which serves up beer-battered fish in a crunchy coating. Much like the U.K. classic, this even-easier at-home recipe just calls for a few classic ingredients like flaky cod, a russet potato, and that all-important lager. For the batter coating, opt for a beer that's lighter as opposed to a heavier stout. In doing so, you'll ensure a crunch that plays well with the fish but won't overwhelm it with too many extra added flavor notes.

6 ounces light beer (such as lager)

1 large egg

½ cup all-purpose flour

1 teaspoon baking powder

½ teaspoon kosher salt

3 cups vegetable oil, for frying

2 (2-ounce) cod pieces

1 large russet potato, skin on, scrubbed and cut into ¼-inch-thick slices

1. Preheat oven to 200°F.
2. In a small mixing bowl, whisk together the beer and egg until frothy. In a separate small mixing bowl, whisk together the flour, baking powder, and salt. Whisk the flour mixture into the beer and egg mixture to create a smooth batter. Let the batter set for about a minute at room temperature, until slightly thickened.
3. In a 3-quart saucepan, heat the vegetable oil to 375°F until it shimmers. Keep the thermometer in the oil to monitor the temperature. Adjust the heat as needed to keep the oil between 350°F and 375°F.
4. Using tongs, dip the fish pieces into the batter, gently shake off excess batter, and carefully lower the fish into the hot oil. Fry the fish for about 5 minutes, turning once, until a golden-brown crust forms on both sides and the internal temperature reaches 145°F.
5. Place the fish on paper towels to absorb the excess oil. Transfer the fish from paper towels to a baking sheet and place in the oven to keep warm while frying the potatoes.
6. Add potato slices to the oil using tongs. Fry about 5 to 6 minutes per side, flipping over when the bottom side of the potato is crisp and golden brown. Cook on the flipped side until crisp and golden brown.

Easy Fish and Chips CONTINUED

Variation Tip: For a lighter option, oven-bake the potatoes at 375°F on a baking sheet sprayed with cooking spray. Bake for about 30 minutes total, flipping halfway through or when the undersides are crisp and golden brown.

Per serving: Calories: 405; Total Fat: 14g; Saturated Fat: 2g; Cholesterol: 93mg; Sodium: 196mg; Carbohydrates: 46g; Fiber: 3g; Protein: 18g

Fisherman's Stew

YIELD: 2 CUPS / PREP TIME: 10 MINUTES / COOK TIME: 15 MINUTES

DAIRY FREE, GLUTEN FREE, NUT FREE, ONE POT

Also known as cioppino, fisherman's stew was traditionally made with whatever was left of the catch of the day—fish like bass or cod, mussels, shrimp, scallops, and squid all jumbled in the pot, every day a different mix. Feel free to improvise with whatever fish you can find affordably and conveniently.

1 tablespoon extra-virgin olive oil

¼ cup chopped yellow onion

½ minced garlic clove

1 cup bottled clam juice

¼ cup white cooking wine or Chardonnay

6 scrubbed littleneck clams

4 ounces cod, cut into bite-size pieces

¼ pound small raw shrimp, peeled and deveined

1 large plum tomato, skinned, seeded, and roughly chopped

2 fresh thyme sprigs or ½ teaspoon dried thyme

½ teaspoon kosher salt

½ cup fresh spinach

¼ cup fresh arugula

1. Heat a 3-quart saucepan over medium heat for 1 minute. Drizzle in the oil and heat until it shimmers, about 1 minute. Add the onion and garlic and sauté until translucent, about 2 minutes.

2. Stir in the clam juice and wine. Bring to a boil over medium-high heat. Add the clams and cod to the pot, and boil over medium-high heat for 1 minute. Reduce heat to medium and continue boiling for 3 minutes, or until the clams open and the fish is opaque.

3. Add the shrimp, tomatoes, thyme, salt, spinach, and arugula to the pot and simmer over medium heat for an additional 2 to 3 minutes, until greens are gently wilted and shrimp are opaque. If using fresh thyme sprigs, remove them from the pan.

Accompaniment Tip: Homemade crusty garlic bread goes well with this seafood-packed stew. Heat broiler on high. Cut a steak roll in half and spread lightly with butter. Top each side with ½ teaspoon garlic powder, ½ teaspoon dried oregano, and 1 tablespoon grated Parmesan cheese. Broil until the bread toasts, butter melts, and cheese browns, about 2 minutes.

Per serving: Calories: 487; Total Fat: 18g; Saturated Fat: 3g; Cholesterol: 306mg; Sodium: 694mg; Carbohydrates: 15g; Fiber: 3g; Protein: 57g

Pesto Salmon

YIELD: 1 SERVING / PREP TIME: 5 MINUTES / COOK TIME: 20 MINUTES

NUT FREE, ONE POT, QUICK MEAL

When I'm undecided on a dinner, pesto, with its romantic origins in Italy, always seems to suit. Its fresh basil and punchy garlic base uplifts chicken, pasta, pork, and vegetables. And on fish, what a treat! I like this powerfully flavored salmon served over wilted greens or sautéed zucchini.

1 (4-ounce) salmon fillet, skin removed

1½ cups fresh basil

1 peeled garlic clove

2 tablespoons grated Parmesan cheese

⅛ teaspoon kosher salt

⅛ teaspoon freshly ground black pepper

1 tablespoon extra-virgin olive oil

Cooking spray

1. Preheat oven to 350°F.
2. Spray baking sheet with cooking spray and place the fish on the sheet.
3. Chop the basil and garlic into fine pieces in a food processor. Grind the cheese, salt, and pepper with the basil garlic mixture into a paste in the food processor.
4. With the food processor running, drizzle the olive oil into the basil mixture and process until pesto forms a thick paste.
5. Coat the fish with half the pesto sauce using a plastic spatula. Bake uncovered for 20 minutes. The fish should be cooked when the center is light pink and flaky. The internal temperature should reach 145°F. Serve the salmon with the remaining pesto on the side if desired.

Accompaniment Tip: Make a quick spinach side dish to go with the salmon. Heat 1 teaspoon vegetable oil in a small sauté pan or skillet over medium heat for about 1 minute until it shimmers. Sauté 2 cups baby spinach in the oil until wilted, about 2 minutes. Drizzle the spinach with 1 teaspoon lemon juice.

Per serving: Calories: 434; Total Fat: 35g; Saturated Fat: 8g; Cholesterol: 72mg; Sodium: 264mg; Carbohydrates: 5g; Fiber: 1g; Protein: 27g

Scallops and Couscous Casserole

YIELD: 2 CUPS / PREP TIME: 10 MINUTES / COOK TIME: 35 MINUTES

BAKE AND SERVE, DAIRY FREE, NUT FREE, QUICK MEAL

Scallops are naturally lower in saturated fat, so you can indulge with a bit of bacon in this recipe. Adding to the ease, this casserole calls for bay scallops, which are smaller than sea scallops, beige to pink in color, and sweet—and they cook in mere minutes.

2 strips raw bacon

½ cup bay scallops

1 tablespoon chopped green onions

¼ cup low-sodium chicken broth

¼ teaspoon smoked paprika

1 cup water

⅔ cup plain couscous (uncooked)

1. Preheat oven to 350°F.

2. Place bacon flat on an ungreased baking sheet and bake for 15 minutes, or until it crisps and the fat turns white. Transfer the cooked bacon to paper towels to drain for 3 minutes before chopping into bite-size pieces. Pour the bacon grease into a small sauté pan.

3. Heat the bacon grease over medium heat until it glistens, about 3 minutes. Add the scallops and green onions to the pan, turning once, until scallops are lightly browned and onions slightly softened, about 1 minute. Reduce the heat to medium-low, add the broth, paprika, and bacon pieces, and simmer for 3 to 5 minutes, or until until scallops are opaque.

4. In a 1-quart saucepan, heat 1 cup water on high until it boils. Pour the couscous into the boiling water, stir, cover, and remove from the heat. Allow the couscous to sit, covered, for 5 minutes. Fluff couscous gently with a fork to separate grains. Plate couscous and top with scallops.

Solo Storage Tip: Buy frozen scallops and thaw just the amount needed for the recipe.

Per serving: Calories: 780; Total Fat: 24g; Saturated Fat: 8g; Cholesterol: 78mg; Sodium: 594mg; Carbohydrates: 93g; Fiber: 6g; Protein: 42g

Seafood Creole

YIELD: 2 CUPS / PREP TIME: 15 MINUTES / COOK TIME: 25 MINUTES

ONE POT, DAIRY FREE

Bring Mardi Gras home by treating yourself to Seafood Creole, which blends shrimp, bay scallops, and tilapia with a rich tomato sauce. Since this recipe has such an assortment of seafood, take care not to overcook the shrimp and scallops! While delicious and delicate, they can easily turn rubbery if left to simmer too long in this rich and spicy Creole sauce.

1 tablespoon extra-virgin olive oil

¼ cup chopped red or green bell peppers

¼ cup diced yellow onion

¼ cup diced celery

½ teaspoon minced garlic

1 tablespoon vegetable oil

1 tablespoon all-purpose flour

1⅓ cups hot water, divided

¾ cup low-sodium chicken broth, divided

1 tablespoon tomato paste

½ cup canned diced tomatoes, with juices

½ teaspoon Creole seasoning

1 tablespoon lemon juice

1. Heat a medium sauté pan over medium heat for 3 minutes. Add the olive oil and heat until it shimmers, about 1 minute. Add the bell peppers, onions, celery, and garlic and sauté for 3 minutes, or until the vegetables are slightly softened. Transfer the cooked vegetables to a plate.

2. Using the same pan, sauté the vegetable oil and flour over medium heat, stirring constantly until it starts to brown and get bubbly. Add ⅓ cup hot water and stir; it will immediately form a paste. Reduce heat to medium-low, pushing the paste into the center of the pan with a heat-resistant spatula, and slowly stir in 1 cup hot water a little at a time until evenly combined.

3. Add the vegetables back into the pan. Add ½ cup chicken broth, then stir in the tomato paste, tomatoes, Creole seasoning, lemon juice, lemon zest, Worcestershire, hot sauce, and bay leaf. Simmer for 2 minutes on low heat to blend the flavors.

4. Increase the heat to medium-low, then add the tilapia. Simmer the fish for 2 minutes before adding the shrimp and scallops. Fold the shrimp and scallops into the stew and continue cooking for an additional 3 minutes, or until fish and scallops are opaque and shrimp are pink in color. If the sauce is too thick, stir in remaining ¼ cup chicken broth. Remove the bay leaf. Serve over cooked rice, quinoa, or barley.

¼ teaspoon lemon zest

1 teaspoon
Worcestershire sauce

½ teaspoon hot sauce

1 bay leaf

1 (3-ounce) tilapia fillet, cut
into 1-inch pieces

¼ pound raw medium-size
shrimp, peeled and deveined

¼ cup bay scallops

1 cup cooked rice, quinoa,
or barley

Cooking Tip: *Roux* describes the paste created by cooking fat with equal parts flour. A roux thickens sauces and makes them smooth.

Per serving: Calories: 825; Total Fat: 32g; Saturated Fat: 4g; Cholesterol: 362mg; Sodium: 1,227mg; Carbohydrates: 76g; Fiber: 4g; Protein: 58g

Shrimp and Crab Cakes

YIELD: 2 CRAB CAKES / PREP TIME: 15 MINUTES, PLUS 5 MINUTES CHILL TIME /
COOK TIME: 10 MINUTES

DAIRY FREE, MAKE AHEAD, NUT FREE

You do not have to be a Maryland native to make authentic crab cakes. Avoid dryness like an expert with this moisture-adding twist: ground shrimp! Shrimp and Crab Cakes taste great over sautéed greens like Swiss chard, kale, or spinach.

¼ cup small raw shrimp, peeled and deveined

4 ounces (claw, special or backfin) crabmeat

2 teaspoons mayonnaise

½ teaspoon brown mustard

¼ teaspoon seafood seasoning, store bought or homemade (see Baked Fish Fillet, page 76)

½ teaspoon lemon juice

½ teaspoon Worcestershire sauce

½ cup bread crumbs, divided

1 tablespoon vegetable oil

1. In a food processor, grind the shrimp by pulsing until coarsely chopped. (Do not grind into a fine paste.) Fold in the crabmeat and set aside.

2. In a separate medium mixing bowl, stir together the mayonnaise, mustard, seafood seasoning, lemon juice, and Worcestershire. Fold the seafood mixture into the bowl and stir to combine.

3. Mix in the bread crumbs by hand, 1 tablespoon at a time, until just enough bread crumbs are added to hold the mixture together, about ¼ cup total.

4. Shape the mixture into 2 patties about 3 inches wide and ½ inch thick. Patties should be a bit loose but hold shape.

5. Place the remaining bread crumbs on a plate. By hand, turn patties lightly in the bread crumbs to coat evenly. Chill for 5 minutes to help the patties hold shape while frying.

6. Heat the oil in a small sauté pan over medium-low heat until it shimmers, about 1 minute. Fry the patties for 5 minutes per side, flipping them halfway through when the cakes are golden brown, crisp, and firm to the touch.

Variation Tip: For a spicy twist, add 1 teaspoon horseradish, ¼ teaspoon hot sauce, and 1 tablespoon diced roasted red peppers before forming the patties.

Per serving: Calories: 426; Total Fat: 20g; Saturated Fat: 2g; Cholesterol: 151mg; Sodium: 1,112mg; Carbohydrates: 24g; Fiber: 1g; Protein: 36g

Shrimp au Gratin

YIELD: 2 CUPS / PREP TIME: 10 MINUTES / COOK TIME: 30 MINUTES

GOOD FOR LEFTOVERS, NUT FREE

What could be richer than Shrimp au Gratin, which bakes tender shrimp with potatoes into a bubbly delight? For this recipe, I reduced the prep and cooking time by using cooked shrimp. If you have extra time, though, raw shrimp work as well.

1 tablespoon unsalted butter, divided

1 cup peeled and sliced (¼-inch-thick) cooked potatoes

½ cup part-skim shredded Cheddar cheese, divided

2 teaspoons cornstarch

½ cup reduced-fat (2-percent) milk

⅛ teaspoon freshly ground black pepper

½ cup chopped cooked medium shrimp

1. Preheat the oven to 350°F.
2. In a 1½-quart baking dish, melt 1 teaspoon butter in the microwave or oven.
3. Arrange half the potato slices in one layer in the bottom of the dish, slightly overlapping them. Sprinkle ¼ cup of the cheese over the potatoes. Layer the remaining potatoes over the cheese layer.
4. In a 1-quart saucepan, whisk together the cornstarch and milk, until the cornstarch is dissolved.
5. Heat the saucepan over medium-low heat, whisking constantly for 1 minute. Whisk in the remaining 2 teaspoons butter and pepper. Continue cooking the sauce over medium-low heat, whisking constantly until thickened, about 3 to 4 minutes.
6. Fold the shrimp into the sauce until thoroughly mixed. Pour the sauce over the potatoes and sprinkle with remaining ¼ cup cheese. Bake, uncovered for 20 minutes, or until the casserole is thoroughly heated and cheese has melted.

Per serving: Calories: 408; Total Fat: 16g; Saturated Fat: 10g; Cholesterol: 319mg; Sodium: 386mg; Carbohydrates: 29g; Fiber: 2g; Protein: 36g

Shrimp Stir-Fry

YIELD: 2 CUPS / PREP TIME: 15 MINUTES / COOK TIME: 10 MINUTES

DAIRY FREE, NUT FREE, ONE POT, QUICK MEAL

Asian-style flavors shine in this stir-fry with nutty sesame oil, salty soy, and the sharp, refreshing bite of fresh ginger. With its rainbow's worth of vegetables, and easy-to-cook shrimp, this recipe will enliven your taste buds.

½ cup unsalted chicken or vegetable broth

2 teaspoons cornstarch

1 tablespoon vegetable oil

¼ pound small raw shrimp, peeled and deveined

¼ cup chopped broccoli florets

½ cup thinly sliced green cabbage

¼ cup thinly sliced onion

¼ cup thinly sliced carrots

¼ cup thinly sliced red bell pepper

¼ cup snap peas, or snow peas in pods

1 teaspoon sesame oil

1 teaspoon low-sodium soy sauce

½ teaspoon sliced fresh ginger

1. In a small mixing bowl, whisk together the broth and cornstarch until the mixture is smooth with no lumps. Set aside.

2. Heat a medium sauté pan over medium-high heat for about 1 minute. Add the vegetable oil and heat until it shimmers, about 1 minute. Sauté the shrimp, broccoli, cabbage, onions, carrots, bell peppers, and peas, turning the shrimp and vegetables when the shrimp is pink on the pan side, about 2 to 3 minutes.

3. Drizzle in the sesame oil and soy sauce, and add the ginger. Stir, cooking for an additional 2 to 3 minutes, until the vegetables are crisp-tender and the shrimp is pink.

4. Reduce heat to medium and add the cornstarch-and-broth mixture. Simmer for about 1 to 2 minutes until the sauce thickens.

Substitution Tip: Instead of shrimp, substitute ¼ cup seitan. Sauté the seitan with 1 teaspoon teriyaki sauce for about 2 minutes to allow the seitan to absorb the sauce before adding it to the stir-fry.

Per serving: Calories: 317; Total Fat: 20g; Saturated Fat: 2g; Cholesterol: 125mg; Sodium: 1,234mg; Carbohydrates: 19g; Fiber: 4g; Protein: 18g

Teriyaki Tuna

YIELD: 1 SERVING / PREP TIME: 15 MINUTES / COOK TIME: 35 MINUTES

DAIRY FREE, NUT FREE, QUICK MEAL

....

In addition to being a delicious meal for your solo dinner table, tuna is an important source of omega-3 fatty acids, which contain anti-inflammatory and antioxidant properties. In this recipe, the teriyaki sauce punches up the tender tuna steak, as do the beautifully roasted red peppers.

....

½ red bell pepper, seeds and white membrane removed

2 tablespoons lemon juice

1 (4-ounce) yellowfin tuna steak

1 tablespoon vegetable oil

½ teaspoon kosher salt

⅛ teaspoon freshly ground black pepper

1 teaspoon rice vinegar

1 teaspoon granulated sugar

1 teaspoon brown sugar

3 tablespoons soy sauce

½ teaspoon chopped fresh ginger

1 tablespoon cornstarch

2 tablespoons water

1. Set broiler on high and place rack 4 inches from the top oven element with the door kept slightly open.

2. Flatten the bell pepper with your hand. Place the bell pepper skin-side up on a broiler pan or baking sheet. Broil the bell pepper with the oven door slightly open, about 3 to 4 minutes, until skin blackens and the pepper softens. Remove the bell pepper from the oven, wrap it in a paper towel, and let it rest for for about 5 minutes to help steam-loosen the skin.

3. Scrape the loosened skin from the bell pepper, then slice it into strips. In a small mixing bowl, marinate the bell pepper strips in lemon juice.

4. Preheat the oven to 450°F.

5. Place a piece of aluminum foil, about 10 to 12 inches long, on a baking sheet. Rub the tuna steak on both sides with the oil, sprinkle with salt and black pepper, and place the tuna in the center of the aluminum foil. Top with marinated pepper strips. Pull the two foil sides up to meet in the center over the fish. Fold the foil pieces together in about ½-inch intervals toward the fish, forming a packet shape. Fold the foil ends up tightly to keep the juices from escaping.

6. Bake for 15 minutes, or until the tuna flakes easily and the center is light pink to dark pink.

CONTINUED ▸

7. Heat a 1-quart saucepan over medium heat for 1 minute. In a small mixing bowl, whisk together rice vinegar, sugar, brown sugar, soy sauce, and ginger until the brown sugar dissolves. Pour the mixture into the heated saucepan.

8. In a small bowl, dissolve the cornstarch in 2 tablespoons water and add to the pan. Cook over medium heat, whisking constantly until the sauce thickens, about 2 to 3 minutes. Drizzle the sauce over the tuna and bell peppers.

Accompaniment Tip: Orange-ginger carrots pair well with teriyaki. Boil ½ cup water, ¼ cup orange juice, ½ cup baby carrots, and ½ teaspoon minced fresh ginger in a 1-quart saucepan for about 5 minutes until carrots are tender.

Per serving: Calories: 409; Total Fat: 16g; Saturated Fat: 3g; Cholesterol: 66mg; Sodium: 3,064mg; Carbohydrates: 24g; Fiber: 2g; Protein: 39g

Tilapia Italiano

YIELD: 1 SERVING / PREP TIME: 10 MINUTES / COOK TIME: 20 MINUTES

DAIRY FREE, NUT FREE, ONE POT

Lean and inexpensive, tilapia is a reliable go-to fish. Livened up by the Italian-tinged vegetable topping, this Tilapia Italiano makes for one mouthwatering meal.

Cooking spray

1 (4-ounce) tilapia fillet

¼ cup diced zucchini

¼ cup diced red bell peppers

½ cup sliced portobello mushrooms

½ teaspoon kosher salt

¼ teaspoon garlic powder

½ teaspoon Italian seasoning

⅛ teaspoon freshly ground black pepper

1 teaspoon balsamic vinegar

2 teaspoons extra-virgin olive oil

1. Preheat oven to 400°F.

2. Spray a small baking dish with cooking spray. Place the tilapia to one side of the dish, allowing room to add the prepared vegetables beside the fish.

3. Mix the zucchini, bell peppers, mushrooms, salt, garlic powder, Italian seasoning, black pepper, balsamic vinegar, and olive oil together in a small bowl. Pour the vegetable mixture next to the tilapia.

4. Bake for 20 minutes, or until the vegetables are softened and the fish turns white and easily flakes with a fork. Stir the vegetables once, halfway through, to ensure even cooking. Transfer the cooked fish to plate and top with the vegetables.

Substitution Tip: Try substituting fresh or frozen asparagus cuts or fresh broccoli instead of mushrooms.

Per serving: Calories: 262; Total Fat: 14g; Saturated Fat: 3g; Cholesterol: 68mg; Sodium: 643mg; Carbohydrates: 6g; Fiber: 1g; Protein: 31g

Tuna Rice Bowl

YIELD: 1 SERVING / PREP TIME: 15 MINUTES / COOK TIME: 15 MINUTES

DAIRY FREE, NUT FREE, QUICK MEAL

This recipe calls for yellowfin tuna because it is cost effective and easy to find. The flaky tuna partners with crunchy cucumbers and radishes, and perfectly absorbs the lemon, coriander, and cumin essence. For a heart-healthy change, try quinoa or barley instead of rice to accompany the seared fish.

2 tablespoons extra-virgin olive oil, divided

1 (4-ounce) yellowfin tuna steak

½ teaspoon ground coriander

½ teaspoon kosher salt

¼ teaspoon cumin

½ cup sliced cucumber

½ avocado, sliced

¼ cup sliced red radishes

¼ cup snow peas

¼ cup sliced carrots

½ cup cooked rice

1 tablespoon freshly squeezed lemon juice

1. Heat a small sauté pan over medium-high heat for 1 minute. Drizzle 1 tablespoon oil into the pan.
2. Rub both sides of the tuna steak lightly with the remaining 1 tablespoon oil, then sprinkle with coriander, salt, and cumin. Fry the tuna on the first side until the bottom of the fish begins to turn brown, about 6 minutes. At this point, fish should easily loosen and lift from the pan.
3. Sear tuna on other side for 3 minutes with a light red center for medium rare, 5 minutes with a pink center for medium. Rest 5 minutes before slicing.
4. Arrange the tuna, cucumbers, avocado, radishes, snow peas, carrots, and rice in a large bowl. Drizzle fresh lemon juice over the tuna bowl to perk up the flavors.

Substitution Tip: Swordfish is another meaty fish steak to try. Fry swordfish for about 3½ to 4½ minutes per side. Swordfish is done when it easily flakes apart with a fork and is opaque.

Per serving: Calories: 668; Total Fat: 43g; Saturated Fat: 7g; Cholesterol: 50mg; Sodium: 376mg; Carbohydrates: 43g; Fiber: 9g; Protein: 32g

COFFEE-RUBBED STEAK, PAGE 107

CHAPTER SIX

PROTEINS MADE SIMPLE (POULTRY AND MEATS FOR ONE)

C ooking poultry and meat for one can be quick, painless, and cost effective with so many choices and portion sizes available at all different price points. From a taste perspective, you'll be flabbergasted at the extent and variety of tasty options you'll find when crafting these scrumptious meat and poultry meals.

Beef-and-Shrimp Surf and Turf

YIELD: 1 SERVING / PREP TIME: 10 MINUTES / COOK TIME: 25 MINUTES

BAKE AND SERVE, NUT FREE

Filet mignon and lobster may be the classic surf and turf combo, but who says it's the only one? A more relaxed but equally delicious take on this classic pairing is strip steak and shrimp. Using strip steak ensures that the meat will cook evenly alongside the plump, buttery, easy-to-find-and-cook shrimp.

1 (8-ounce) strip steak

½ teaspoon kosher salt

⅛ teaspoon freshly ground black pepper

1 tablespoon vegetable oil

3 tablespoons unsalted butter, divided

¼ cup lemon juice

¼ cup white cooking wine

¼ cup thinly sliced portobello mushrooms

¼ pound small raw shrimp, peeled and deveined

½ teaspoon minced garlic

4 teaspoons thinly sliced chives, divided

¼ cup crushed oyster cracker pieces

⅛ teaspoon seafood seasoning, store bought or homemade (see Baked Fish Fillet, page 76)

1. Preheat oven to 350°F.

2. Season both sides of the steak with salt and pepper. Add oil to an oven-safe medium sauté pan and heat over medium-high heat until it shimmers, about 1 minute. Sear both sides of the steak until golden brown, about 5 minutes per side.

3. Finish cooking the steak in the oven for 5 to 10 minutes until internal temperature is 130°F for medium rare. Transfer the steak to a cutting board to rest for 5 minutes. Cut rested steak into thin slices.

4. In the same pan, heat 1 tablespoon unsalted butter, lemon juice, and cooking wine, scraping to deglaze the bottom of the pan, and cook for 1 minute more.

5. Using a fine sieve, strain the butter sauce into a small sauté pan. Heat the pan over medium heat for 1 minute until butter sauce begins to warm.

6. Sauté the mushrooms and shrimp in butter sauce for about 1 to 2 minutes over medium heat, then add garlic and 2 teaspoons chives. Cook until shrimp turns opaque, mushrooms are browned, and garlic is soft, about 4 more minutes. Set aside and cover with a lid to keep warm.

7. Heat a small sauté pan over medium heat for 1 minute. Melt remaining 2 tablespoons unsalted butter in pan. Stir in oyster cracker pieces and seafood seasoning. Cook until butter is absorbed and cracker pieces are lightly browned, 3 to 4 minutes. Set aside.

8. Layer the mushrooms and shrimp over the steak. Sprinkle with crumbs and remaining 2 teaspoons chives. Drizzle with remaining sauce.

Cooking Tip: For a thicker sauce, add more butter or cook slightly longer to reduce. For a looser sauce, thin with a bit more wine.

Per serving: Calories: 956; Total Fat: 60g; Saturated Fat: 24g; Cholesterol: 332mg; Sodium: 1,674mg; Carbohydrates: 8g; Fiber: 1g; Protein: 80g

Beef Barley Skillet Dinner

YIELD: 1 SERVING / PREP TIME: 15 MINUTES / COOK TIME: 20 MINUTES

DAIRY FREE, GOOD FOR LEFTOVERS, ONE POT

Beef Barley Skillet features tender steak paired with toothsome barley and hearty vegetables. Choose your steak mindfully: Petite sirloin and sirloin are inexpensive, flavorful cuts that cook up tender when braised, while rib eye and strip steaks have a higher fat content, but cook a bit faster than sirloin.

1 tablespoon vegetable oil

1 (8-ounce) steak (petite sirloin, sirloin, rib eye, or strip)

1 teaspoon kosher salt

⅛ teaspoon freshly ground black pepper

½ cup sliced green onions (green and white parts)

½ cup diced carrots

½ cup chopped broccoli

1 teaspoon minced garlic

2 tablespoons chopped red bell peppers

1 cup unsalted beef broth

1 teaspoon dried thyme

½ cup quick-cook barley

1. Heat a medium sauté pan over medium-high heat for 1 minute. Drizzle in the oil and heat until it shimmers, about 1 minute.

2. Season the steak with salt and pepper. Sear the steak on both sides until evenly browned, about 2 minutes per side. Transfer steak to a plate and let it rest for 5 minutes before slicing into strips, reserving the juices. Divide the slices into 2 portions and refrigerate 1 portion in a resealable plastic bag to use later.

3. Add the green onion, carrots, and broccoli to the pan and sauté over medium heat for 1 to 2 minutes. Add the garlic and bell peppers. Cook for another 1 to 2 minutes, or until the vegetables are crisp tender.

4. Return the sliced steak to the pan. Add the broth and thyme, stirring to combine.

5. Bring the steak, vegetables, and broth to a boil over medium heat. Stir in the barley. Cover and reduce heat to low and simmer for about 10 minutes or until steak is cooked and barley is tender.

Solo Storage Tip: Most steaks are portioned as 8- to 12-ounce pieces. By buying these larger packages, then saving half for another meal, your choice is both economical and time-saving.

Per serving: Calories: 590; Total Fat: 24g; Saturated Fat: 12g; Cholesterol: 170mg; Sodium: 810mg; Carbohydrates: 33g; Fiber: 7g; Protein: 57g

Beefy Mac and Cheese

YIELD: 2 CUPS / PREP TIME: 20 MINUTES / COOK TIME: 15 MINUTES

BAKE AND SERVE, NUT FREE

With this recipe, we leave boxed versions of mac and cheese in the dust, but not at the expense of convenience. Should you have it on hand, use leftover beef from roasts, steaks, or shredded pot roast.

Cooking spray

½ cup dry macaroni (such as elbows, shells, or penne)

1 cup whole milk

1 tablespoon cornstarch

½ teaspoon dry mustard

1 tablespoon unsalted butter

4 ounces shredded part-skim Cheddar cheese

1 cup chopped cooked beef

¼ cup chopped cooked bacon

2 tablespoons thinly sliced green onion (green parts)

1. Preheat oven to 350°F.
2. Spray an 8-by-8-inch baking dish with cooking spray.
3. Cook the macaroni according to package directions. Drain.
4. Heat a 2-quart saucepan over medium heat for about 1 minute. Whisk together milk, cornstarch, and mustard in a small bowl. Add to the warm pan. Stir in the butter.
5. Bring the mixture to a boil over medium-low heat. Boil about 1 minute, reduce heat to low, and simmer, stirring constantly until thickened, about 2 minutes. Remove from heat and whisk in the cheese until the sauce is smooth, about 1 minute. Cheese does not need to be completely melted.
6. Fold the beef and macaroni into the cheese sauce. Pour the combined mixture into the prepared baking dish.
7. Bake until the cheese is melted and thoroughly heated to 165°F, about 15 minutes. The cheese sauce will be glossy, and the top of the casserole lightly browned in spots. To serve, sprinkle with chopped bacon and green onion.

Accompaniment Tip: Prepare a simple side dish of ½ cup cooked baby carrots or ½ cup cooked broccoli florets to add some nutrients.

Per serving: Calories: 1,006; Total Fat: 50g; Saturated Fat: 24g; Cholesterol: 197mg; Sodium: 1,411mg; Carbohydrates: 54g; Fiber: 2g; Protein: 80g

Chicken Meatballs and Spaghetti

YIELD: 1 SERVING / PREP TIME: 15 MINUTES / COOK TIME: 25 MINUTES

GOOD FOR LEFTOVERS

These chicken meatballs are a lighter twist on the classic beef, pork, and veal combination. This fresh take updates the tomato sauce with a garlic butter sauce for exciting variety.

¼ pound ground chicken

1 tablespoon shredded fresh Asiago or Parmesan cheese

½ teaspoon minced fresh parsley

¼ cup chopped green onion

½ teaspoon dried basil

⅛ teaspoon kosher salt

⅛ teaspoon freshly ground black pepper

¼ cup plain panko bread crumbs, divided

1 tablespoon vegetable oil

2 ounces dry spaghetti (about ¼ of an 8-ounce box)

2 tablespoons unsalted butter

2 tablespoons extra-virgin olive oil

½ teaspoon minced garlic

1. Preheat oven to 350°F.

2. In a medium mixing bowl, mix together by hand the ground chicken, cheese, parsley, onion, basil, salt, and pepper until thoroughly combined.

3. Mix in the bread crumbs 1 tablespoon at a time, adding just enough bread crumbs to hold the mixture together. By hand, shape the mixture into 4 loosely formed meatballs.

4. Heat a medium oven-safe sauté pan over medium-high heat for about 1 minute. Drizzle the vegetable oil into the pan and heat until it shimmers, about 1 minute.

5. Reduce the pan to medium heat. Fry the meatballs, turning quickly to coat with oil on all sides. Reduce heat to medium-low and continue turning the meatballs to brown all sides. Transfer the pan to the oven.

6. Bake the browned meatballs for about 10 minutes until the internal temperature reaches 165°F. Reduce oven to 175°F to keep cooked meatballs warm until sauce and pasta are ready.

7. Cook spaghetti according to package directions. Drain.

8. Heat a small sauté pan over medium heat for 1 minute. Melt butter with olive oil in heated pan until oil is hot and butter is slightly foamy, about 1 to 2 minutes.

9. Sauté garlic in oil and butter mixture over medium heat for about 2 to 3 minutes, or until it softens and browns. Plate the spaghetti, top with meatballs, and drizzle with sauce.

Variation Tip: Try a fresh zucchini, butternut, or yellow squash spiralized noodle as a low-calorie alternative to pasta.

Per serving: Calories: 1015; Total Fat: 76g; Saturated Fat: 25g; Cholesterol: 161mg; Sodium: 305mg; Carbohydrates: 55g; Fiber: 4g; Protein: 32g

Chicken Piccata

YIELD: 1 SERVING / PREP TIME: 15 MINUTES / COOK TIME: 25 MINUTES

NUT FREE, ONE POT

My take on this Italian classic freshens it up with briny capers and freshly squeezed lemon juice in the sauce. It's a breeze to make and one of my all-time favorites. Use extra capers in pickling recipes, omelets, deviled eggs, and salmon and cream cheese bagels!

½ cup all-purpose flour

¼ teaspoon kosher salt

⅛ teaspoon freshly ground black pepper

2 tablespoons unsalted butter

2 tablespoons extra-virgin olive oil

1 (4-ounce) skinless, boneless chicken breast

2 tablespoons freshly squeezed lemon juice

¼ cup unsalted chicken broth

2 tablespoons rinsed, brined capers

1 tablespoon chopped fresh parsley

1. In a medium bowl, mix together the flour, salt, and pepper. Place the mixture on a plate for easy coating.

2. Heat a small sauté pan over medium heat for about 1 minute. Add butter and olive oil and simmer until slightly frothy.

3. Dredge the chicken in the seasoned flour, gently shaking off the excess flour before adding to the pan. Fry the chicken on medium heat for about 5 minutes per side, until evenly browned. Transfer the browned chicken to a plate.

4. Add lemon juice, chicken broth, and capers to the pan, stirring to combine. Return the chicken to the pan, add the parsley, and simmer on low heat for about 10 minutes, or until the chicken reaches 160°F and the sauce thickens.

5. Cover the pan with a lid and remove the pan from the heat. Let the pan rest, covered, for 5 minutes before plating to allow juices to settle back into the chicken. Plate the chicken and spoon the remaining sauce on top.

Per serving: Calories: 861; Total Fat: 55g; Saturated Fat: 22g; Cholesterol: 126mg; Sodium: 727mg; Carbohydrates: 56g; Fiber: 3g; Protein: 34g

Chicken Stew

YIELD: 3 CUPS / PREP TIME: 15 MINUTES / COOK TIME: 30 MINUTES

DAIRY FREE, GOOD FOR LEFTOVERS, ONE POT, NUT FREE

On cold winter days when I was a kid, I loved a dinner of warming chicken stew with my family. In this slightly more grown-up version, delicate baby greens add a slightly bitter flavor that balances the acid from tomatoes and plays nicely with the chicken.

1 tablespoon vegetable oil

¼ cup chopped celery

¼ cup baby carrots

1 tablespoon chopped onion

1 cup unsalted chicken broth

½ cup ½-inch pieces potatoes

½ teaspoon minced garlic

½ teaspoon kosher salt

½ cup baby greens (such as spinach, arugula, mustard, collard greens, or kale)

½ cup chopped cooked chicken breast

½ cup canned diced tomatoes, with juices

1. Heat a 2-quart saucepan on medium-high heat for about 1 minute. Add the oil and heat until it shimmers, about 1 minute.

2. Sauté the celery, carrots, and onion until crisp-tender, about 2 minutes.

3. Reduce the heat to medium. Add the broth, potatoes, garlic, and salt and bring to a boil. Reduce the heat and cook for about 10 minutes, or until the potatoes are almost cooked.

4. Stir in the greens, chicken, and tomatoes, and thoroughly heat over medium heat, about 5 minutes more. Greens will be wilted and vegetables tender.

Variation Tip: Try sweet potatoes, turnips, or beets instead of tomatoes. Cut vegetables into roughly 1-inch pieces. Follow the recipe and add these vegetables in step 3.

Per serving: Calories: 328; Total Fat: 17g; Saturated Fat: 2g; Cholesterol: 54mg; Sodium: 466mg; Carbohydrates: 20g; Fiber: 5g; Protein: 25g

Chipotle Rib Eye

YIELD: 1 STEAK / PREP TIME: 25 MINUTES / COOK TIME: 30 MINUTES

GLUTEN FREE, NUT FREE

Chipotle Rib eye is a smoky heat–seasoned steak with a bit of bite and whole lot of flavor. To save time, I use canned chipotle peppers in adobo sauce for the smoky heat flavor. Caramelized onions balance out the heat with a bit of sweet.

1 tablespoon unsalted butter

½ cup sliced yellow onion

1 tablespoon vegetable oil

1 (4- to 6-ounce) rib eye steak

½ teaspoon kosher salt

⅛ teaspoon freshly ground black pepper

¼ teaspoon garlic powder

½ teaspoon ground cumin

½ teaspoon paprika

¼ teaspoon ground cinnamon

1 tablespoon adobo sauce from 1 can adobo chipotles

1 chipotle pepper from canned adobo chipotles

1. Heat a small sauté pan over medium heat for 1 minute. Melt the butter in the heated pan.
2. Add the butter and onions and sauté over medium-low heat for 20 minutes, or until the onions turn golden brown and reduce by half.
3. Heat another small sauté pan over medium heat for 1 minute. Add oil and heat until it shimmers about 1 minute.
4. Season the steak with salt and pepper. Fry over medium-high heat for 5 minutes per side for medium rare (125°F to 130°F internal temperature before resting). Flip the steak with tongs when a browned crust has formed and the steak easily releases from the pan. Fry the second side for an additional 5 to 6 minutes or until browned.
5. Using tongs, transfer the cooked steak to a cutting board or plate and allow the steak to rest for 5 to 10 minutes before cutting to allow juices to redistribute into the meat.
6. In a small mixing bowl, whisk together the garlic powder, cumin, paprika, ground cinnamon, and adobo sauce.
7. Scrape seeds from the chipotle pepper. Chop the pepper finely. Fold the chopped pepper into the sauce. Spoon the chipotle sauce over the steak. Top with caramelized onions.

Cooking Tip: Remember to wear gloves and/or thoroughly wash hands when coming in contact with hot peppers of any kind.

Per serving: Calories: 578; Total Fat: 51g; Saturated Fat: 21g; Cholesterol: 111mg; Sodium: 688mg; Carbohydrates: 9g; Fiber: 4g; Protein: 22g

Coffee-Rubbed Steak

YIELD: 1 STEAK / PREP TIME: 5 MINUTES / COOK TIME: 15 MINUTES

DAIRY FREE, GOOD FOR LEFTOVERS, NUT FREE, QUICK MEAL

When combined with beef, coffee adds an earthy taste that is out of this world. I first heard of adding ground coffee to recipes in the late 1990s when home roasters and spice mills were popping up everywhere. What an eye opener! Though the finest grind of coffee is best for this super easy Coffee-Rubbed Steak, a coarser grind will also work.

2 teaspoons kosher salt

1 teaspoon chili powder

1 teaspoon freshly ground black pepper

1 teaspoon smoked paprika

1 teaspoon finely ground coffee

½ teaspoon thyme

1 (8-ounce) strip steak

1 tablespoon vegetable oil

1. Preheat oven to 350°F.

2. In a resealable plastic bag, combine the salt, chili powder, pepper, paprika, coffee, and thyme.

3. Brush both sides of the steak with the oil. Sprinkle 1 teaspoon of the coffee seasoning on each side of the steak and rub in vigorously using clean hands.

4. Heat a small oven-safe sauté pan over medium heat for 1 minute. Add the seasoned steak. Fry over medium-high heat for about 2 minutes per side. Flip the steak with tongs when a brown crust starts to form and the steak easily releases from the pan. Fry the second side for about 2 minutes, until a brown crust begins to form.

5. Finish cooking the steak in the oven for about 5 to 10 minutes, or as necessary until the internal temperature is 130°F for medium rare using a digital thermometer. Let the steak rest for 5 to 10 minutes before cutting.

Variation Tip: This 8-ounce steak will make 2 servings. Reheat leftover steak in a small sauté pan with ¼ cup beef broth over medium heat for 1 to 2 minutes per side, until thoroughly heated.

Per serving: Calories: 609; Total Fat: 46g; Saturated Fat: 13g; Cholesterol: 170mg; Sodium: 267mg; Carbohydrates: 1g; Fiber: 1g; Protein: 44g

Easy Fajitas

YIELD: 2 MINI FAJITAS / PREP TIME: 10 MINUTES / COOK TIME: 15 MINUTES / MARINATING TIME: 20 MINUTES

NUT FREE, ONE POT

Endlessly flexible, fajitas are the perfect custom-tailored meal for one that works perfectly with beef or chicken.

1 (4-ounce) sliced ¼-inch-thick steak or chicken breast

2 tablespoons vegetable oil, divided

1 tablespoon freshly squeezed lime juice

½ teaspoon homemade fajita seasoning (see tip) or prepackaged mix

½ teaspoon minced garlic

½ cup ¼-inch-thick slices red bell pepper

½ cup ¼-inch-thick slices green bell pepper

½ cup ¼-inch-thick slices yellow onion

Cooking spray

2 (6-inch) flour tortillas

Taco sauce, shredded cheese, sour cream, salsa, or guacamole, for topping (optional)

1. In a 1-quart resealable plastic bag, place protein, 1 tablespoon oil, lime juice, fajita seasoning, and garlic. Marinate for 20 minutes or more in the refrigerator.
2. Heat a medium sauté pan over medium heat. Add 1 tablespoon oil and heat until it shimmers, about 1 minute.
3. Add the protein, bell peppers, and onions to the pan. Turn protein and peppers halfway through cooking time, about 4 minutes for steak and 6 minutes for chicken.
4. Fry the protein until it is completely cooked, an additional 4 to 5 minutes for medium-rare steak, or 6 to 8 minutes for fully cooked chicken. Cooked chicken should reach an internal temperature of 165°F.
5. Spray a medium sauté pan with cooking spray. Heat the pan over medium heat for 1 minute.
6. Heat the tortillas in the pan for 1 minute per side to warm them. Serve with taco sauce, shredded cheese, sour cream, salsa, and guacamole, if desired.

Substitution Tip: To make your own fajita seasoning combine 1½ teaspoons salt, 1 teaspoon dried oregano, 1 teaspoon chili powder, ½ teaspoon ground cumin, 1 teaspoon garlic powder, ½ teaspoon coriander, and ½ teaspoon paprika. Store unused seasoning in a resealable plastic bag for future use.

Per serving: Calories: 618; Total Fat: 36g; Saturated Fat: 3g; Cholesterol: 72mg; Sodium: 693mg; Carbohydrates: 44g; Fiber: 5g; Protein: 31g

Hickory BBQ Chicken Legs

YIELD: 2 PIECES CHICKEN / PREP TIME: 15 MINUTES / COOK TIME: 50 MINUTES

DAIRY FREE, NUT FREE, ONE POT

I cannot resist BBQ chicken, and with these Hickory BBQ Chicken Legs, I think you'll be right there with me. Here, smoked salt contributes a perfect smoky flavor you're bound to love.

½ cup tomato sauce

2 teaspoons Worcestershire sauce

2 teaspoons red wine vinegar

1 tablespoon brown sugar

¼ teaspoon smoked salt

2 teaspoons vegetable oil

2 bone-in chicken thighs or drumsticks, skin removed

1. Preheat oven to 375°F.
2. In a 1-quart saucepan, whisk together the tomato sauce, Worcestershire, red wine vinegar, brown sugar, and smoked salt.
3. Simmer over medium-low heat, whisking occasionally, for 5 minutes or until the brown sugar has dissolved. Remove from the heat and divide into 2 small bowls, one for coating the raw chicken and the second for a dipping sauce.
4. Drizzle the oil into a small baking dish. Add the chicken pieces brush them liberally with the sauce.
5. Bake the chicken for 40 to 50 minutes, using tongs to turn once about halfway through cooking. The chicken is done when a meat thermometer pierced into the center registers 180°F and the meat shows signs of pulling away from the bone.

Accompaniment Tip: Steamed or lightly boiled carrots, broccoli, or cauliflower sprinkled with fresh lemon juice balance well with this smoky-sweet chicken.

Per serving: Calories: 415; Total Fat: 18g; Saturated Fat: 3g; Cholesterol: 190mg; Sodium: 1091mg; Carbohydrates: 18g; Fiber: 2g; Protein: 46g

Honey Mustard Chicken Breast

YIELD: 1 SERVING / PREP TIME: 10 MINUTES / COOK TIME: 15 MINUTES

DAIRY FREE, GOOD FOR LEFTOVERS, NUT FREE, ONE POT, QUICK MEAL

Mustard has been used as a condiment for thousands of years, and in this recipe the pungency of Dijon is balanced by the sweetness of honey. I panfry the chicken and add the sauce after cooking to keep the flavors precise and clean.

1 tablespoon vegetable oil

1 (4-ounce) skinless, boneless chicken breast

1 tablespoon honey

1 teaspoon Dijon mustard

1 teaspoon mayonnaise

¼ teaspoon kosher salt

1. Heat a small sauté pan over medium heat for 1 minute. Add the oil and heat until it shimmers, about 1 minute.

2. Add the chicken and fry for 7 minutes on the first side, until browned. Flip when a crust forms and chicken easily releases from the pan. Continue frying on the second side for 8 to 10 minutes, until evenly browned. When properly cooked, the interior of the chicken will register 165°F using a digital thermometer. Transfer the cooked chicken to a plate. Cover with aluminum foil to keep warm.

3. In a small bowl, whisk together the honey, mustard, mayonnaise, and salt. Brush it onto the cooked chicken breast. Serve over cooked rice or noodles, or your favorite lightly steamed vegetable.

Variation Tip: Make extra chicken and sauce for a next-day lunch sandwich. Wrap the chicken and store the sauce separately in the refrigerator.

Per serving: Calories: 339; Total Fat: 19g; Saturated Fat: 1g; Cholesterol: 74mg; Sodium: 300mg; Carbohydrates: 19g; Fiber: 0g; Protein: 24g

Honey-Sriracha Pork and Beans

YIELD: 1 CUP / PREP TIME: 10 MINUTES / COOK TIME: 10 MINUTES

DAIRY FREE, GOOD FOR LEFTOVERS, NUT FREE, QUICK MEAL

An iconic hot sauce thanks to its garlic-packed spice and recognizable rooster, Sriracha is so popular it's moved beyond the fridge and into popular culture. With this recipe, you can join the throngs of Sriracha fans and indulge in a satisfying and filling pork and beans dish. This dish can be served hot or cold, so it makes a great take-along picnic or work lunch.

2 tablespoons tomato sauce

½ teaspoon Sriracha

1 teaspoon honey

½ teaspoon Worcestershire sauce

½ teaspoon red wine vinegar

½ cup cooked shredded pork loin

½ cup canned cannellini beans, rinsed and drained

1. Heat a 2-quart saucepan over medium heat for about a minute. Whisk together the tomato sauce, Sriracha, honey, Worcestershire, and red wine vinegar in the pan and simmer over medium-low heat for 5 minutes.
2. Stir in the pork and beans. Cook another 4 to 5 minutes to thoroughly heat to 165°F, and serve immediately for a warm version.
3. For a cool version, place the pork and beans in a refrigerator-safe container, uncovered, to cool. Cover when completely cold. Honey-Sriracha Pork and Beans will keep in the refrigerator for 3 days.

Variation Tip: Add ½ cup of your favorite chopped leafy green, such as kale or spinach, to the beans for a nutrient-packed boost.

Per serving: Calories: 250; Total Fat: 3g; Saturated Fat: 1g; Cholesterol: 53mg; Sodium: 249mg; Carbohydrates: 29g; Fiber: 7g; Protein: 27g

Juicy Lucy Beef Burger

YIELD: 1 BURGER / PREP TIME: 10 MINUTES / COOK TIME: 15 MINUTES

NUT FREE, QUICK MEAL

The Juicy Lucy Beef Burger's name and concept are claimed by two bars in Minneapolis. This is no mere afterthought of cheese melted atop an already cooked burger; it's an indulgent infusion of juicy beef with cheese.

1 slice cheese (such as American or Cheddar)

4 ounces ground beef (80 percent lean)

½ teaspoon kosher salt

¼ teaspoon minced garlic

½ teaspoon Worcestershire sauce

⅛ teaspoon freshly ground black pepper

Cooking spray

1 hamburger bun, toasted

4 dill pickle slices

1. Cut the cheese slice in half, then in half again, to form 4 squares. Place the pieces on top of each other to form a stack.

2. In a large bowl, combine ground beef, salt, garlic, Worcestershire, and pepper together by hand and form two equal patties. Press each piece into roughly ¼-inch-thick patties.

3. Place the cheese stack in the center of 1 of the patties. Top it with the second patty and pinch the edges together to close. Shape the patty by hand into a burger.

4. Heat a griddle or small sauté pan sprayed with cooking spray over medium heat for about 1 minute.

5. Fry the burger for 6 to 8 minutes, or until evenly browned. Flip after about 6 minutes, or when a browned crust forms. Avoid putting pressure on burgers with spatulas because this will cause the burger to lose juices and cheese.

6. Fry the burger on the second side for an additional 6 to 8 minutes, until a brown crust forms and the internal temperature reaches 160°F. Serve it on the toasted hamburger bun with pickles and your favorite condiments.

Per serving: Calories: 481; Total Fat: 29g; Saturated Fat: 12g; Cholesterol: 76mg; Sodium: 843mg; Carbohydrates: 25g; Fiber: 1g; Protein: 31g

Meat Lover's Calzone

YIELD: 1 SERVING / PREP TIME: 15 MINUTES / COOK TIME: 20 MINUTES

GOOD FOR LEFTOVERS, NUT FREE, ONE POT

I love making calzones as a weekend treat. One dough round makes four individual calzones, and the filling possibilities are endless—but be careful to seal them tightly, as filling will leak out if you leave any holes.

Cooking spray

¼ cup all-purpose flour

¼ premade pizza dough

2 tablespoons whole-milk ricotta cheese

1 chopped cooked breakfast sausage link

1 slice deli ham

1 tablespoon bacon bits

¼ cup shredded part-skim mozzarella cheese

1 large egg

1 teaspoon water

1. Preheat oven to 425°F. Spray a baking sheet lightly with cooking spray.

2. Sprinkle flour onto a cutting board or other clean, flat surface. Roll the dough into a 6-inch square, about ¼-inch thick. Spread the ricotta onto the dough, leaving about a ½-inch border. Place the sausage, ham, and bacon bits on top of half the ricotta to leave room to fold the dough over the filling. Sprinkle the mozzarella cheese over the meat.

3. In a small bowl, whisk together the egg and water. Brush a light coating of egg wash over the bare edges of the calzone. Fold the dough over the filling so the edges meet, pinching tightly to seal.

4. Place the calzone on the baking sheet. Brush the top of the dough lightly with the remaining egg wash. Make 2 or 3 small 1-inch cuts on top to allow steam to escape.

5. Bake the calzone for 20 minutes or until golden brown and dough is thoroughly cooked.

Solo Storage Tip: For later use and easy separation, wrap individual calzones in wax paper and place in a freezer bag.

Per serving: Calories: 746; Total Fat: 30g; Saturated Fat: 11g; Cholesterol: 262mg; Sodium: 1,321mg; Carbohydrates: 79g; Fiber: 5g; Protein: 43g

Mini Turkey Meatloaf

YIELD: 1 SERVING / PREP TIME: 10 MINUTES / COOK TIME: 45 MINUTES

GOOD FOR LEFTOVERS

Meatloaf's reputation ranks low on the scale of exciting meal options, but it's time to give this dish the appreciation it deserves as nourishing comfort food. My Mini Turkey Meatloaf switches up the traditional recipe by using poultry instead of beef, farina instead of bread crumbs, and some seasonings for an added kick. The farina ensures a smoother, less coarse texture.

Cooking spray

½ pound lean ground turkey

¼ cup farina or plain bread crumbs

1 large egg

¼ cup diced onion

1 teaspoon minced garlic

2 teaspoon Worcestershire sauce

½ teaspoon kosher salt

2 teaspoon dried parsley

¼ teaspoon cayenne pepper

1. Preheat oven to 350°F.
2. Line a baking sheet with foil. Spray with cooking spray.
3. In a medium mixing bowl, place the ground turkey, farina, egg, onion, garlic, Worcestershire, salt, parsley, and cayenne pepper. Mix by hand to form a large ball. Form the ball into a loaf, about 3x5 inches, and place on the baking sheet.
4. Bake for 25 minutes. Remove it from the oven and slice ½-inch intervals into the loaf. Bake an additional 15 minutes, or until the turkey is thoroughly cooked and reaches 150°F internal temperature using a digital thermometer.

Variation Tip: Heat chopped leftover meatloaf in your favorite prepared spaghetti sauce to serve over your favorite pasta.

Per serving: Calories: 427; Total Fat: 17g; Saturated Fat: 4g; Cholesterol: 322mg; Sodium: 751mg; Carbohydrates: 17g; Fiber: 2g; Protein: 51g

Orange-Maple Smoked Pork Chops

YIELD: 1 SERVING / PREP TIME: 10 MINUTES / COOK TIME: 15 MINUTES

NUT FREE, QUICK MEAL

Lean pork can be a satisfying, nutrient-dense protein to add to your diet. Orange-Maple Smoked Pork Chops, are glazed with a combination of salty, sweet, and a bit of spice from the horseradish and mustard. If it's more convenient, and your palate prefers, you can substitute apple juice for orange, or try buckwheat honey instead of standard honey.

1 tablespoon unsalted butter

3 tablespoons orange juice

½ teaspoon horseradish

1 tablespoon honey

1 tablespoon maple syrup

½ tablespoon brown mustard

¼ teaspoon salt

1 (4- to 6-ounce) boneless smoked pork chop

1. Preheat oven to 375°F.
2. In a small microwave-safe dish, microwave the butter for about 20 seconds to soften. Whisk in the orange juice, horseradish, honey, maple syrup, mustard, and salt. Spread the glaze over the smoked pork chop.
3. Bake the glazed smoked pork chop in a small, shallow baking dish for 15 to 20 minutes, until thoroughly heated to an internal temperature of 140°F and glaze has thickened.

Cooking Tip: The thickness of smoked pork chops varies greatly between butchers and brands. Decrease cook time for thinner chops by about 5 minutes. The internal temperature should reach 140°F.

Per serving: Calories: 456; Total Fat: 18g; Saturated Fat: 10g; Cholesterol: 119mg; Sodium: 1,841mg; Carbohydrates: 44g; Fiber: 0g; Protein: 30g

Pork Chop with Pineapple Salsa

YIELD: 1 SERVING / PREP TIME: 30 MINUTES / MARINATING TIME: 30 MINUTES / COOK TIME: 20 MINUTES

DAIRY FREE, MAKE AHEAD, NUT FREE, ONE POT

For a bit of heat with a bit of sweet, try this succulent recipe. Panfrying the pork ensures an evenly browned chop that's moist and juicy. If your schedule allows, make the pineapple salsa the night before, giving the flavors time to marry. For a vegan option, exchange the pork chop for 4 ounces of seitan. Fry the seitan for 4 to 5 minutes per side until golden brown.

½ cup canned crushed pineapple, drained

1 tablespoon diced red bell peppers

1 teaspoon diced red onion

½ teaspoon diced jalapeño, seeds and membrane removed

1 teaspoon lime juice

½ teaspoon kosher salt, divided

½ teaspoon chopped fresh cilantro

¼ cup all-purpose flour

⅛ teaspoon freshly ground black pepper

2 teaspoons vegetable oil

1 thin bone-in or boneless pork chop

1. In a medium mixing bowl, stir together the pineapple, bell peppers, onions, jalapeño, lime juice, ¼ teaspoon salt, and cilantro. Marinate in the refrigerator for at least 30 minutes, or overnight.

2. In a small mixing bowl, stir together the flour, remaining ¼ teaspoon salt, and black pepper. Place the flour mixture on a shallow plate for easier coating.

3. Heat a small sauté pan over medium heat for 1 minute. Add the oil and heat until it shimmers, about 1 minute.

4. Dredge both sides of the pork in the seasoned flour, shake off the excess flour, and add the pork to the hot pan.

5. Fry the pork about 4 minutes per side. The pork should be golden brown when finished and the internal temperature should reach 145°F. Top with the salsa before serving.

Accompaniment Tip: For even more crunch, add ½ cup chopped raw broccoli to the salsa.

Per serving: Calories: 511; Total Fat: 23g; Saturated Fat: 6g; Cholesterol: 55mg; Sodium: 640mg; Carbohydrates: 49g; Fiber: 4g; Protein: 30g

Sausage and Peppers

YIELD: 1 SERVING / PREP TIME: 15 MINUTES / COOK TIME: 25 MINUTES

DAIRY FREE, NUT FREE, ONE POT

The smell of sausage cooking brings back childhood memories. Sausage and Peppers is one of my favorite meals. I grew up eating this dish with country pork sausage over rice, yet it's truly a global meal, with interpretations of it ranging from Eastern Europe to South America. An inexpensive, delicious, and accessible dish, I recommend serving it over rice or farro so the grains can soak up the flavors of the sausage and peppers.

1 tablespoon vegetable oil

½ pound country pork sausage, casings removed, cut into 1-inch pieces

½ cup sliced green bell peppers

½ cup sliced red bell peppers

½ cup sliced onions

½ teaspoon minced garlic

1 teaspoon dried basil

1 teaspoon Worcestershire sauce

½ cup cooked rice, farro, or couscous

1. Heat a medium sauté pan over medium heat. Add the oil to the pan and heat until it shimmers, about 1 minute.

2. Add the sausage, bell peppers, onions, garlic, basil, and Worcestershire sauce to the pan and cover. Cook over medium heat for 20 to 25 minutes or until the peppers are soft and the sausage is no longer pink. Spoon over cooked rice, farro, or couscous.

Variation Tip: Replace half the amount of bell peppers with sliced fennel, which adds an anise flavor that goes well with sausage.

Per serving: Calories: 1034; Total Fat: 75g; Saturated Fat: 28g; Cholesterol: 120mg; Sodium: 1,466mg; Carbohydrates: 42g; Fiber: 4g; Protein: 49g

Sheet Pan Chicken and Roasted Vegetables

YIELD: 1 SERVING / PREP TIME: 15 MINUTES / COOK TIME: 30 MINUTES

BAKE AND SERVE, DAIRY FREE, ONE POT

Sheet pan dinners are enduring and classic because they're an easy way to make a main dish and sides in one pan, hence why they're beyond ideal for the solo cook! The chicken thighs in this recipe cook fast at high heat and stay juicy. I also recommend heating the sheet pan before baking, which helps food cook more quickly.

2 skinless and boneless chicken thighs

½ cup red potato, skin on, cut into 1-inch pieces

½ cup 1-inch pieces broccoli

¼ cup baby carrots

½ teaspoon kosher salt

½ teaspoon Italian seasoning

1 tablespoon vegetable oil

1. Preheat oven to 425°F.
2. Heat an empty sheet pan in the oven for 5 minutes. Fill a 1-gallon resealable bag with the chicken, potato, broccoli, carrots, salt, Italian seasoning, and oil. Toss to coat the chicken and vegetables with oil and seasonings.
3. Remove the pan from the oven using oven mitts or hot pads and place it on a heat-resistant surface. Spread the prepared chicken and vegetables onto the hot sheet pan in an even, single layer.
4. Bake for 30 to 40 minutes until vegetables are crisped and browned and chicken registers 180°F using a digital thermometer.

Variation Tip: Try onions, parsnips, snap peas, and cauliflower for different flavors.

Per serving: Calories: 450; Total Fat: 24g; Saturated Fat: 5g; Cholesterol: 192mg; Sodium: 560mg; Carbohydrates: 14g; Fiber: 4g; Protein: 46g

Turkey Cutlets

YIELD: 1 SERVING / PREP TIME: 10 MINUTES / COOK TIME: 15 MINUTES

DAIRY FREE, GOOD FOR LEFTOVERS, NUT FREE, ONE POT, QUICK MEAL

Quick-cooking turkey cutlets are an excellent choice for a weeknight meal. What's more, they're a lean and healthy option that pairs well with gravy or can be shredded for barbecue. They also make great sandwich stuffers or salad toppings anytime you need a light yet nourishing protein boost.

4 ounces (¼- to ½-inch thickness) turkey cutlets

½ teaspoon kosher salt

⅛ teaspoon pepper

¼ teaspoon garlic powder

¼ teaspoon dried thyme

1 tablespoon vegetable oil

1 tablespoon fresh squeezed lemon juice

1. Season cutlets on both sides with salt, pepper, garlic powder, and thyme.
2. Heat a small sauté pan over medium heat. Add the oil to the pan and heat until it shimmers.
3. Fry the seasoned turkey for about 3 minutes per side to brown. Flip the turkey when browned and easily removes from pan. Fry flipped side about 3 minutes. Cook until turkey is no longer pink and registers 165°F, about 6 to 7 minutes total. Drizzle with fresh squeezed lemon juice.

Variation Tip: For a southwestern flair, try substituting ¼ teaspoon paprika and ⅛ teaspoon cumin for thyme and omit the lemon juice.

Per serving: Calories: 271; Total Fat: 16g; Saturated Fat: 2g; Cholesterol: 68mg; Sodium: 367mg; Carbohydrates: 5g; Fiber: 0g; Protein: 27g

BERRY GALETTE, PAGE 123

CHAPTER SEVEN

TREAT YOURSELF (DESSERTS FOR ONE)

Don't think of dessert as an indulgence, but rather as a well-deserved cap on your day. Grabbing a cookie or cupcake is fine on occasion, but the world of single-serve desserts offers much more. Whether you crave a tart, fruity treat, or a gooey chocolate bite, this chapter will speak to you.

Apple Kugel

YIELD: 1 SERVING / PREP TIME: 15 MINUTES / COOK TIME: 45 MINUTES

BAKE AND SERVE

While kugels are sweet and savory, my Apple Kugel marries tender noodles with cottage cheese, sour cream, and semisweet apple enhanced by cinnamon, ginger, and nutmeg. The smell of these warming spices baking with the apples is pure perfume!

1 cup dry wide noodles

2 tablespoons melted, cooled unsalted butter

¼ cup granulated sugar

2 ounces light sour cream

2 ounces low-fat cottage cheese

1 teaspoon vanilla extract

½ teaspoon cinnamon

⅛ teaspoon ground ginger

⅛ teaspoon nutmeg

1 large beaten egg

¼ cup cored, peeled, chopped McIntosh or other semisweet apple

Cooking spray

1. Preheat oven to 350°F.

2. Cook the noodles according to the package directions. Drain and place in a large mixing bowl.

3. In a separate large mixing bowl, combine the butter, sugar, sour cream, cottage cheese, vanilla, cinnamon, ginger, and nutmeg. Fold in the egg and apples. Pour over the noodles and stir to coat evenly.

4. Spray a 1½-quart baking dish with cooking spray. Fold in the kugel mixture. Bake for 45 minutes or until the custard is set and the noodles start to brown. Fully cooked custard will register to an internal temperature of 150°F and an inserted tip of a butter knife will come out clean.

Variation Tip: Add dried fruit, such as raisins or cranberries, for a different taste and texture.

Per serving: Calories: 759; Total Fat: 33g; Saturated Fat: 19g; Cholesterol: 292mg; Sodium: 357mg; Carbohydrates: 96g; Fiber: 4g; Protein: 21g

Berry Galette

YIELD: 1 SERVING / PREP TIME: 15 MINUTES / COOK TIME: 30 MINUTES

BAKE AND SERVE

This rustic take on pie has a freeform look, with its pastry sides folded over to keep the lush fruit from leaking out. Liven it up with toasted and chopped walnuts, fresh sliced bananas, or chocolate if you like. While refrigerated pie dough provides convenience, your favorite homemade dough works, too.

½ cup mixed berries (such as blueberries, raspberries, and chopped strawberries)

1 teaspoon lemon juice

½ teaspoon vanilla extract

¼ cup granulated sugar

2 teaspoons cornstarch

⅛ teaspoon salt

1 refrigerated pie crust, cut into 6-inch round

1 large egg, beaten

1 teaspoon water

1 tablespoon turbinado sugar

1. Preheat oven to 425°F.
2. Line a baking pan with parchment paper. In a medium mixing bowl, mix together the berries, lemon juice, vanilla, sugar, cornstarch, and salt. Set aside.
3. Using a slotted spoon, fill the pie crust with the berry mixture, leaving the edges empty to fold over. Pull up the dough edges, overlapping if necessary. Gently press to hold together, crimping the dough lightly with your fingers.
4. In a small bowl, whisk together the egg and water. Brush the galette with the egg wash and sprinkle with the turbinado sugar. Bake for 30 minutes, or until the crust is browned, berries are bubbling, and the dough is fully cooked.

Cooking Tip: The longer berries sit, the more juice will collect and soak through the dough, so use the berry mixture promptly.

Per serving: Calories: 668; Total Fat: 26g; Saturated Fat: 5g; Cholesterol: 186mg; Sodium: 775mg; Carbohydrates: 101g; Fiber: 2g; Protein: 10g

Blueberry Trifle

YIELD: 1 CUP / PREP TIME: 10 MINUTES / COOK TIME: 10 MINUTES /
CHILL TIME: 15 MINUTES (OPTIONAL)

NO BAKE

This rich dessert's blueberries boast a high level of antioxidants, proving just why you should indulge in this single-serve delight. Marrying vanilla yogurt and homemade whipped cream with soft pieces of pound cake and flavorful berries, this perfectly sized trifle hits all the right notes for a deliciously sweet ending. Feel free to switch up the blueberries and add in your favorite berries, like tart raspberries or juicy strawberries, for an entirely different fruity take. In case you're worried about your whipped cream falling flat, read ahead to my tip for foolproof peaks.

1 cup cubed pound cake, divided

½ cup blueberries, fresh or frozen

¼ cup water, divided

2 tablespoons granulated sugar

½ teaspoon cornstarch

2 tablespoons low-fat vanilla yogurt

2 teaspoons homemade whipped cream (see tip)

1. Place half the pound cake cubes into a heat-safe container. A 7-ounce ramekin or small mason jar is ideal.

2. In a 1-quart saucepan, bring the blueberries, 3 tablespoons water, and sugar to a boil over medium heat. Reduce the heat to simmer and cook for 5 minutes, whisking constantly, until the blueberries soften and sauce begins to gel. Remove from the heat.

3. In a small mixing bowl, combine the cornstarch and remaining 1 tablespoon water. Whisk the cornstarch into the blueberries. Return it to the stovetop and cook over medium heat for 1 minute, stirring constantly to thicken the sauce.

4. Place half the blueberry mixture on top of the pound cake. In a separate small mixing bowl, whisk together the yogurt and whipped cream. Fold half the yogurt on top of the blueberries. Top the yogurt with the remaining pound cake cubes. Pour the remaining blueberries over the pound cake, and top with remaining yogurt.

5. Eat immediately; for a colder dessert, chill 15 minutes before serving.

Substitution Tip: Homemade whipped cream is useful for a wide range of desserts. Chill a medium mixing bowl in the freezer for 20 minutes. Pour 1 cup cold heavy cream into the chilled bowl. Whisk in ¼ cup powdered sugar and ¼ teaspoon vanilla extract. Using a rotary or electric mixer on medium speed, whip until until firm peaks form, about 5 minutes. Turn off the mixer as soon as stiff peaks form and the whipped cream pulls away from the side of the bowl. Overmixing will produce butter.

Per serving: Calories: 342; Total Fat: 10g; Saturated Fat: 6g; Cholesterol: 103mg; Sodium: 203mg; Carbohydrates: 62g; Fiber: 2g; Protein: 5g

Chocolate Chip Cookie Bar

YIELD: 1 SERVING / PREP TIME: 10 MINUTES / COOK TIME: 18 MINUTES / COOLING TIME: 5 MINUTES

NUT FREE, ONE POT

According to food lore, the chocolate chip cookie was invented in 1938 by the chef who owned the Toll House Inn in Massachusetts. Even today, very little beats a homemade chocolate chip cookie—except maybe my homemade Chocolate Chip Cookie Bar! This one-dish wonder bakes in a single ramekin, making it easier to top your cookie bar with whipped cream, ice cream, sprinkles, or anything else your sweet tooth desires.

Cooking spray

2 tablespoons melted unsalted butter

1 tablespoon granulated sugar

1 tablespoon brown sugar

⅛ teaspoon vanilla extract

¼ cup all-purpose flour

⅛ teaspoon baking soda

⅛ teaspoon kosher salt

2 tablespoons semisweet chocolate chips

1. Preheat oven to 375°F.
2. Spray a 7-ounce ramekin with cooking spray.
3. In a medium mixing bowl, whisk together the butter, sugar, brown sugar, and vanilla until sugars are dissolved.
4. In a separate bowl, whisk together the flour, baking soda, and salt. Fold the wet ingredients into the dry ingredients. Stir in the chocolate chips. Fold the dough into the ramekin.
5. Bake for 15 to 18 minutes or until the surface is firm to the touch and brown. Cool for 5 minutes on a wire rack before serving. Sprinkle with assorted toppings, if desired.

Substitution Tip: For those less tempted by chocolate, substitute the chocolate chips with raisins, dried cranberries, or your favorite chopped and toasted nuts.

Per serving: Calories: 539; Total Fat: 31g; Saturated Fat: 21g; Cholesterol: 60mg; Sodium: 453mg; Carbohydrates: 63g; Fiber: 2g; Protein: 3g

Cinnamon-Chocolate Brownie

**YIELD: 1 BROWNIE / PREP TIME: 10 MINUTES / COOK TIME: 25 MINUTES /
COOLING TIME: 5 MINUTES**

BAKE AND SERVE, NUT FREE, ONE POT

The warming aroma of cinnamon enhances the already-delicious taste of the chocolate in this simple treat. I opt for unsweetened chocolate instead of cocoa because assembling and baking in the same ramekin works better with melted chocolate than potentially messy cocoa powder.

**1½ tablespoons
unsalted butter**

**½ ounce unsweetened
chocolate**

¼ cup granulated sugar

⅛ teaspoon vanilla extract

1 large egg yolk

**2 tablespoons
all-purpose flour**

⅛ teaspoon kosher salt

⅛ teaspoon baking soda

¼ teaspoon cinnamon

1. Preheat oven to 350°F.
2. Melt the butter and chocolate in a 7- to 8-ounce microwave-safe ramekin in the microwave on high for 5-second intervals until the chocolate is completely melted.
3. Stir in the sugar and vanilla. Cool the chocolate mixture slightly, about 1 minute, before adding the egg yolk so as not to curdle it.
4. In a separate bowl, mix together the flour, salt, baking soda, and cinnamon. Fold the dry mixture into the wet mixture until evenly combined.
5. Place the ramekin directly onto the oven rack. Bake the brownie for about 25 minutes, or until inserted toothpick comes out clean. Serve in the ramekin. Allow the brownie to cool slightly before eating, about 3 to 5 minutes. Cooling longer will help firm the brownie, if desired.

Cooking Tip: Oven- and microwave-safe ramekins make baking for one so much easier. Individual-size desserts bake with less mess and easy cleanup.

Per serving: Calories: 523; Total Fat: 29g; Saturated Fat: 17g; Cholesterol: 256mg; Sodium: 584mg; Carbohydrates: 67g; Fiber: 3g; Protein: 6g

Cookies-and-Cream Cake

**YIELD: 1 SERVING / PREP TIME: 10 MINUTES / COOK TIME: 1 TO 2 MINUTES /
COOLING TIME: 5 MINUTES**

NUT FREE, ONE POT

I have zero willpower when it comes to certain sweets, and for me, chocolate sandwich cookies take the cake, so to speak. In my Cookies-and-Cream Cake, dark, crisp chocolate cookie pieces mix with creamy bites of filling, all baked into a convenient single-serve mug cake, making an easy dessert with even easier cleanup! Remember to let the cake cool a bit before eating so it doesn't have a gummy texture.

**4 tablespoons
all-purpose flour**

¼ teaspoon baking powder

4 teaspoons granulated sugar

3 tablespoons whole milk

2 teaspoons vegetable oil

¼ teaspoon vanilla extract

2 chocolate sandwich cookies

¼ cup homemade whipped cream (optional, see Blueberry Trifle, page 125)

1. In a 7-ounce microwave-safe ramekin, mix together the flour, baking powder, sugar, milk, oil, and vanilla.

2. Place the cookies in a resealable sandwich bag and roll over the sealed bag with a rolling pin to crush the cookies. Stir the crushed cookies into the cake batter.

3. Microwave for 1 minute. If the cake is too runny, microwave at 10-second intervals until it is firmly set and baked. Let cool for 3 to 5 minutes before eating. Top with whipped cream, if desired.

Variation Tip: Add a bit more chocolate flavor to the cake by stirring in a teaspoon of semisweet chocolate chips before microwaving.

Per serving: Calories: 392; Total Fat: 15g; Saturated Fat: 3g; Cholesterol: 5mg; Sodium: 117mg; Carbohydrates: 60g; Fiber: 2g; Protein: 6g

Cranberry Rice Pudding

YIELD: 1 SERVING / PREP TIME: 10 MINUTES / COOK TIME: 20 MINUTES

5 INGREDIENTS OR FEWER, ONE POT

A relatively healthy dessert option, my version of the classic and comforting rice pudding uses almond milk instead of traditional cream. Almond milk is a good source of calcium and vitamin E with no cholesterol, and it adds a delightfully nutty taste and creamy texture in contrast to the tart cranberries.

1¼ cup unsweetened almond milk, divided

⅓ cup cooked rice (such as white or basmati)

1 tablespoon granulated sugar

¼ teaspoon cinnamon

1 tablespoon dried cranberries

1. In a 1-quart saucepan, combine 1 cup almond milk, rice, sugar, cinnamon, and cranberries.

2. Bring to a boil over medium heat, stirring constantly. Boil for 1 minute. Reduce heat to low. Simmer, stirring often until rice is tender and liquid is absorbed, about 20 minutes.

3. Remove from the heat and add the remaining ¼ cup almond milk. Fold the pudding into a serving dish. Enjoy warm or cold.

Substitution Tip: Leftover brown rice works well in place of freshly cooked basmati or white rice.

Per serving: Calories: 355; Total Fat: 7g; Saturated Fat: 0g; Cholesterol: 0mg; Sodium: 226mg; Carbohydrates: 74g; Fiber: 5g; Protein: 7g

Mini Strawberry Graham Pie

YIELD: 1 PIE / PREP TIME: 10 MINUTES

NO BAKE, NUT FREE

These little pies are my toned-down take on a local favorite called Mile High Strawberry Pie, which earned its name because the baker piled jellied strawberries "a mile high." In order to keep the berries in place, the baker covered the pie with gobs of whipped cream. Our single-serving portion measures slightly less than a mile high, but it's every bit as satisfying.

½ cup graham cracker crumbs

1 tablespoon granulated sugar

2 tablespoons melted unsalted butter

¼ cup strawberry preserves

½ cup fresh sliced strawberries

¼ cup homemade whipped cream (see Blueberry Trifle, page 125)

1. In a small mixing bowl, stir together the graham cracker crumbs and sugar. Add the butter and stir to combine.
2. Firmly press down the crumb mixture into the bottom of a 7-ounce ramekin, then work the mixture up the sides, pressing tightly as you go. Keep the crust around ¼ inch thick. If it is too dry, add more melted butter to the mixture.
3. In a small mixing bowl, stir together the strawberry preserves with fresh strawberries. Fold the filling into the ramekin in a single, even layer. Top with whipped cream.

Variation Tip: Try changing the fruit to juicy, ripe peaches and peach preserves boosted with a sprinkle of cinnamon.

Per serving: Calories: 758; Total Fat: 37g; Saturated Fat: 23g; Cholesterol: 101mg; Sodium: 385mg; Carbohydrates: 105g; Fiber: 4g; Protein: 4g

Mocha Fudge

YIELD: 1 POUND FUDGE / PREP TIME: 10 MINUTES / COOK TIME: 15 MINUTES / CHILL TIME: 1 HOUR

GOOD FOR LEFTOVERS, MAKE AHEAD, NUT FREE

This luscious Mocha Fudge recipe blends semisweet chocolate with a hint of coffee into a gooey, irresistible delight. Mocha Fudge keeps fresh for about a week if cut and wrapped tightly in wax paper and then plastic wrap, and even longer if frozen.

Cooking spray

¼ cup evaporated milk

½ cup granulated sugar

1 tablespoon unsalted butter

⅛ teaspoon salt

½ cup semisweet chocolate chips

½ cup mini marshmallows

1 teaspoon instant coffee granules

1. Spray a 1½-quart baking dish with cooking spray.
2. In a 2-quart saucepan, whisk together the evaporated milk, sugar, butter, and salt. Bring to a boil over medium heat and continue cooking, stirring constantly for 5 minutes, or until thickened.
3. Remove the pan from the heat. Whisk in the chocolate chips, marshmallows, and instant coffee until evenly combined.
4. Pour the fudge into the prepared baking dish. Spread into a single, even layer using a heat-resistant rubber spatula.
5. Chill uncovered until firm before serving, about 1 hour.

Variation Tip: Add chopped walnuts or sliced almonds for a bit of contrasting crunch.

Per serving (⅛ recipe): Calories: 155; Total Fat: 6g; Saturated Fat: 4g; Cholesterol: 6mg; Sodium: 55mg; Carbohydrates: 25g; Fiber: 0g; Protein: 2g

No-Bake Blueberry Cheesecake

YIELD: 1 SERVING / PREP TIME: 20 MINUTES / CHILL TIME: 2 HOURS

MAKE AHEAD, NO BAKE

Simple No-Bake Blueberry Cheesecake is a great summertime treat, easy to assemble, and tantalizing for one. Adding fresh fruit, like juicy blueberries, lends flavor, balance, and vitamins to this dessert, while the fruit helps cut the inherent richness of the creamy cheesecake filling. Check to be sure the graham cracker crust is suitably set before filling so that your cheesecake holds its shape. Feel free to mix up the fruit, too, should you want to try a mixed-berry no-bake delight!

Cooking spray

½ cup graham cracker crumbs

¼ cup plus 3 tablespoons granulated sugar, divided

2 tablespoons melted unsalted butter

½ cup fresh blueberries

2 tablespoons water

½ teaspoon lemon juice

4 ounces cream cheese, softened

½ teaspoon vanilla extract

4 ounces whipped cream (see Blueberry Trifle, page 125) (optional)

1. Spray a 7- to 8-ounce ramekin generously with cooking spray. In a small bowl, mix together the graham cracker crumbs and 1 tablespoon sugar. Add the butter and stir to combine. Firmly press down the crumb mixture into the bottom of the ramekin, then work the mixture up the sides, pressing tightly as you go. Keep the crust around ¼ inch thick. If it is too dry, add more melted butter to the mixture. Refrigerate the crust to let it harden before filling, at least 1 hour.

2. In a 1-quart saucepan, bring the blueberries, ¼ cup sugar, water, and lemon juice to a boil. Reduce to medium-low heat and simmer, stirring constantly, until sauce thickens, about 5 minutes. Pour thickened sauce into a heatproof container. Allow it to cool at room temperature for about 5 minutes, then refrigerate until serving time.

3. In a small mixing bowl, beat the cream cheese, remaining 2 tablespoons sugar, and vanilla until smooth. Spoon the filling into the chilled graham cracker crust.

4. Refrigerate for 1 hour, until mixture thickens, before eating. Top with blueberry sauce when cheesecake is firm and ready to eat.

Substitution Tip: Substitute a rich chocolate cookie crust for the graham cracker crust. Place 5 chocolate sandwich cookies in a resealable plastic bag and, using a rolling pin, crush cookies thoroughly. Mix the cookie crumbs with 1 tablespoon melted butter. Press the crumb mixture on the bottom and up the sides of the ramekin. Chill for 30 minutes before filling with cream cheese filling.

Per serving: Calories: 1,146; Total Fat: 66g; Saturated Fat: 41g; Cholesterol: 185mg; Sodium: 711mg; Carbohydrates: 133g; Fiber: 4g; Protein: 12g

Peanut Butter Pie

YIELD: 1 SERVING / PREP TIME: 10 MINUTES / COOK TIME: 5 MINUTES / CHILL TIME: 2 HOURS
5 INGREDIENTS OR FEWER, NO BAKE

As wildly popular as peanut butter is with Americans, this peanut butter pie takes it to an unbelievably easy level, with a smooth, creamy, crustless version using instant pudding. You can eat it as a pudding or dress it up to make a full-on sundae, adding mini peanut butter cups, chopped peanuts, or whipped cream.

¼ cup smooth peanut butter

½ cup whole milk

½ small package instant vanilla pudding

½ cup whipped cream (see Blueberry Trifle, page 125)

1. In a small mixing bowl, add the peanut butter and gradually stir in the milk, blending until smooth. Whisk in the instant pudding mix until smooth, about 2 minutes. Fold in the whipped cream.

2. Spoon the mixture into a pint-size mason jar or similar glass. Refrigerate for at least 2 hours before eating.

Storage Tip: Use a freezer-safe container if you like a firmer pie filling. Freeze the container for about 2 hours before enjoying.

Per serving: Calories: 846; Total Fat: 59g; Saturated Fat: 23g; Cholesterol: 94mg; Sodium: 796mg; Carbohydrates: 66g; Fiber: 4g; Protein: 21g

Piña Colada Blondies

YIELD: 4 BLONDIES / PREP TIME: 15 MINUTES / COOK TIME: 30 MINUTES

BAKE AND SERVE, ONE POT

My Piña Colada Blondies add a tropical flair to traditional blondies and are an entirely new dessert take on that classic cocktail. The result? A soft, chewy, and exotic cross between a brownie and a cookie. Well-drained pineapple cuts the sweetness while toasted coconut adds crunch—but sorry, they're rum free!

1 tablespoon melted unsalted butter

½ cup flour

¼ teaspoon baking powder

⅛ teaspoon salt

¼ cup unsalted butter

¼ cup granulated sugar

⅛ cup brown sugar

1 large egg yolk

2 ounces chopped fresh dark cherries

¼ cup crushed canned pineapple, drained

½ cup toasted, shredded sweetened coconut

1. Preheat the oven to 350°F.
2. Line a small baking pan with aluminum foil, allowing a few inches to hang off the ends. Brush foil with 1 tablespoon melted butter and set aside.
3. In a small mixing bowl, whisk together the flour, baking powder, and salt.
4. In a separate bowl, mix together ¼ cup butter, granulated sugar, and brown sugar. Stir in the egg yolk.
5. Using a rubber spatula, fold the wet mixture into the dry mixture. Spread the dough evenly over the bottom of the greased pan. Dot it with cherry pieces. Using a butter knife, swirl the cherry pieces into the dough.
6. Bake for 30 minutes, or until an inserted toothpick comes out clean. Allow the pan to cool for 15 minutes before removing the blondies with foil intact. Lift the foil by the overlap "handles" and set on a rack to finish cooling.
7. Cut the cooled blondies into the desired sizes. Top them with crushed pineapple and toasted coconut.

Variation Tip: Keep this blondie tropical but change it up a bit by replacing the pineapple with diced mangos and adding macadamia nuts.

Per serving: Calories: 329; Total Fat: 18g; Saturated Fat: 13g; Cholesterol: 38mg; Sodium: 81mg; Carbohydrates: 42g; Fiber: 2g; Protein: 3g

Pumpkin Pie

**YIELD: 1 SERVING / PREP TIME: 20 MINUTES / COOK TIME: 20 MINUTES /
CHILL TIME: 1 TO 2 HOURS**

NUT FREE

Early colonial settlers in New England may have made a form of this ubiquitous Thanksgiving favorite, but this version bears little resemblance to the original. It is made with tassie dough, which contains cream cheese and makes for a moister crust than traditional pie dough.

¼ cup plus 2 tablespoons softened unsalted butter, divided

3 ounces cream cheese, divided

2 tablespoons granulated sugar

½ cup all-purpose flour

2 tablespoons pumpkin purée

1 tablespoon brown sugar

1 large egg

⅛ teaspoon pumpkin pie spice

1. Preheat the oven to 350°F.
2. Beat together ¼ cup butter, 1½ ounces of cream cheese, and sugar. Add the flour to form a soft dough ball. Refrigerate for 5 minutes to chill for easier handling. Divide the chilled dough into 2 balls. Press the balls into 2 ungreased large muffin cups, filling the bottom and sides.
3. Beat together the remaining 2 tablespoons butter, remaining 1½ ounces cream cheese, pumpkin purée, and brown sugar until fluffy. Beat in the egg and pumpkin pie spice. Divide the filling between the two crusts. Bake for 15 to 20 minutes, until the filling is set and the crust is browned. Do not overbake.
4. Cool on a wire rack for 5 minutes before removing. Cool the pies to room temperature, then chill for 1 to 2 hours before serving.

Per serving: Calories: 1,358; Total Fat: 101g; Saturated Fat: 68g; Cholesterol: 460mg; Sodium: 327mg; Carbohydrates: 92g; Fiber: 3g; Protein: 20g

Raisin Bread Pudding

YIELD: 1 SERVING / PREP TIME: 15 MINUTES / COOK TIME: 30 MINUTES

BAKE AND SERVE, ONE POT

Bread pudding was once a way to use leftover stale bread, but this version takes fresh raisin bread and raises the stakes. This recipe makes it simple with all of the cinnamon and seasonings baked into the bread already. When buying bread, look for unsliced raisin bread so you can cut it as thick as you like. Regardless of thickness, the custard will flow into all the nooks and crannies.

1 teaspoon butter, softened

1 cup 1-inch pieces raisin bread

1 large egg

1 large egg yolk

2 tablespoons brown sugar

½ cup whole milk

1. Preheat oven to 375°F.
2. Using the softened butter, thoroughly grease a small baking dish (1½-quart size).
3. Arrange the bread pieces loosely in the greased dish. In a small mixing bowl, whisk together the egg, egg yolk, brown sugar, and milk. Pour the custard over the bread.
4. Bake for about 30 minutes, or until the custard sets and the top is golden brown. Test the custard for doneness by inserting a butter knife into the custard part. The knife will come out clean when the custard is fully cooked.

Variation Tip: Try using leftover cinnamon rolls instead of raisin bread for a deeply cinnamon-flavored pudding.

Per serving: Calories: 376; Total Fat: 17g; Saturated Fat: 7g; Cholesterol: 416mg; Sodium: 293mg; Carbohydrates: 41g; Fiber: 1g; Protein: 16g

Vanilla Mug Cake

YIELD: 1 SERVING / PREP TIME: 10 MINUTES / COOK TIME: 2 MINUTES

BAKE AND SERVE

This mug cake is a quick but tantalizing sweet-tooth satisfier, and a perfect way to resolve an emergency treat craving. Enjoy as is or switch up the cake's flavor with different extracts to make it a lemon, orange, or root beer–tinged treat. It's delicious either with a quick icing or a dollop of whipped cream. Just remember that the mug will be hot, so use caution when removing it from the microwave and while eating.

4 tablespoons all-purpose flour

½ teaspoon baking powder

3 tablespoons granulated sugar

2 teaspoons unsalted butter, softened

4 tablespoons reduced-fat (2-percent) milk

½ teaspoon vanilla

Cooking spray

1. In a small mixing bowl, mix together the flour, baking powder, and sugar.

2. In a separate small mixing bowl, mix the butter, milk, and vanilla. Add the wet mixture to the dry mixture. Stir to combine.

3. Lightly spray a large (12-ounce or larger) microwave-safe mug with cooking spray, then add the batter. Microwave the mug on high for 1 minute 30 seconds until thoroughly baked to a firm, but not runny, texture. Test for doneness by inserting a toothpick into the center; it will come out clean when cake is properly baked. Eat immediately.

Variation Tip: For a chocolate-infused version, replace 1 teaspoon of flour with 1 teaspoon of cocoa powder.

Per serving: Calories: 360; Total Fat: 10g; Saturated Fat: 6g; Cholesterol: 25mg; Sodium: 33mg; Carbohydrates: 64g; Fiber: 1g; Protein: 5g

MEASUREMENT CONVERSIONS

VOLUME EQUIVALENTS (LIQUID)

US STANDARD	US STANDARD (OUNCES)	METRIC (APPROXIMATE)
2 tablespoons	1 fl. oz.	30 mL
¼ cup	2 fl. oz.	60 mL
½ cup	4 fl. oz.	120 mL
1 cup	8 fl. oz.	240 mL
1½ cups	12 fl. oz.	355 mL
2 cups or 1 pint	16 fl. oz.	475 mL
4 cups or 1 quart	32 fl. oz.	1 L
1 gallon	128 fl. oz.	4 L

OVEN TEMPERATURES

FAHRENHEIT	CELSIUS (APPROXIMATE)
250°F	120°C
300°F	150°C
325°F	165°C
350°F	180°C
375°F	190°C
400°F	200°C
425°F	220°C
450°F	230°C

VOLUME EQUIVALENTS (DRY)

US STANDARD	METRIC (APPROXIMATE)
⅛ teaspoon	0.5 mL
¼ teaspoon	1 mL
½ teaspoon	2 mL
¾ teaspoon	4 mL
1 teaspoon	5 mL
1 tablespoon	15 mL
¼ cup	59 mL
⅓ cup	79 mL
½ cup	118 mL
⅔ cup	156 mL
¾ cup	177 mL
1 cup	235 mL
2 cups or 1 pint	475 mL
3 cups	700 mL
4 cups or 1 quart	1 L

WEIGHT EQUIVALENTS

US STANDARD	METRIC (APPROXIMATE)
½ ounce	15 g
1 ounce	30 g
2 ounces	60 g
4 ounces	115 g
8 ounces	225 g
12 ounces	340 g
16 ounces or 1 pound	455 g

THE DIRTY DOZEN AND THE CLEAN FIFTEEN™

A nonprofit environmental watchdog organization called Environmental Working Group (EWG) looks at data supplied by the US Department of Agriculture (USDA) and the Food and Drug Administration (FDA) about pesticide residues. Each year it compiles a list of the best and worst pesticide loads found in commercial crops. You can use these lists to decide which fruits and vegetables to buy organic to minimize your exposure to pesticides and which produce is considered safe enough to buy conventionally. This does not mean they are pesticide-free, though, so wash these fruits and vegetables thoroughly. The list is updated annually, and you can find it online at EWG.org/FoodNews.

DIRTY DOZEN™

1. strawberries	5. apples	9. pears
2. spinach	6. grapes	10. tomatoes
3. kale	7. peaches	11. celery
4. nectarines	8. cherries	12. potatoes

† Additionally, nearly three-quarters of hot pepper samples contained pesticide residues.

CLEAN FIFTEEN™

1. avocados	6. papayas*	11. cauliflower
2. sweet corn*	7. eggplants	12. cantaloupes
3. pineapples	8. asparagus	13. broccoli
4. sweet peas (frozen)	9. kiwis	14. mushrooms
5. onions	10. cabbages	15. honeydew melons

* A small amount of sweet corn, papaya, and summer squash sold in the United States is produced from genetically modified seeds. Buy organic varieties of these crops if you want to avoid genetically modified produce.

REFERENCES

I Value Food. "Cooking for One with Zero Waste." www.ivaluefood.com /resources/cooking-eating/cooking-for-one-with-zero-waste.

Montana State University Extension. "Cooking for One or Two Fact Sheet." www.buyeatlivebetter.org/main_documents/factsheets/factsheet%20 cooking-for%20one.pdf.

PBS. "Cooking for One." www.pbs.org/food/theme/cooking-for-one.

University of Nebraska–Lincoln. "Cooking Healthy Meals for One or Two—A Checklist." www.food.unl.edu/fnh/cooking-for-1-or-2.

University of Nebraska–Lincoln. "Reducing the Size of Recipes." www.food.unl .edu/reducing-size-recipes-0.

University of Rhode Island. "Simple Meals for One or Two." www.web.uri.edu /snaped/recipes/simple-meals-for-one-or-two.

USDA. "Eat Right When Money's Tight." www.snaped.fns.usda.gov /nutrition-education/nutrition-education-materials/eat-right-when -moneys-tight.

RESOURCES

This reliable four-piece mini measuring set has wonderfully useful small-measurement beakers:
www.oxo.com/categories/cooking-and-baking/mix-measure/measuring-cups-spoons/4-piece-mini-measuring-beaker-set-459.html

This 3.5-cup food processor features pulse control and two speeds, plus easy access to add liquid:
www.kitchenaid.com/countertop-appliances/food-processors/processors/p.kfc3516ga.html

Sur La Table is a wonderful resource for individual 7-ounce ramekins:
www.surlatable.com

Bed Bath & Beyond has an ideal selection of larger ramekins (like this set of 4- to 8-ounce ramekins):
www.bedbathandbeyond.com/store/product/porcelain-ramekins-set-of-4/1013469199

This useful article will help you determine if pans are oven safe:
www.leaf.tv/articles/how-to-determine-if-pans-are-oven-safe

This is a great comparison guide for purchasing skillets and frying pans:
www. foodal.com/kitchen/pots-pots-skillets-guides-reviews/guides/best-frying-pans/#stainless-steel

I recommend this 8-inch oven-safe skillet:
www.cuisinart.com/shopping/cookware/skillets-fry-pan/422-20

INDEX

ACKNOWLEDGMENTS

I want to thank Rockridge Press and Callisto Media for their support as I brought *The Cooking for One Cookbook* to life. Special thanks to my managing editor, Jesse Aylen, and developmental editor, Caryn Abramowitz, for their guidance and dedication to helping me deliver the best version possible.

Many thanks also to my friends James Ruhf and Maureen Reynolds Zella for believing in me, standing by me, and encouraging me throughout my career to better my skills. I also need to thank my fans and followers at *Cindy's Recipes and Writings* for their many positive comments and support.

Special thanks go out to my mentor, Isabel Reis Laessig, Family Foodie and Sunday Supper Movement creator, who gave me the opportunity to broaden my reach on social media, partner with outstanding brands, and meet many fellow food enthusiasts whom I have grown to love dearly.

I can't forget to acknowledge my family who, over the years, have helped me on various food-related business opportunities, from live events to video to travel ventures. All those endeavors led to the opportunity to create this cookbook. Thank you, Amanda, Rob, Cecilyn, Malcolm, and Tom for all of your help, love, and support.

ABOUT THE AUTHOR

 Cindy Kerschner grew up with a respect for food, both for how it's grown and for its value as a resource that should not be wasted. In time, that love grew into culinary classes and to her becoming a Master Gardener. Today, Cindy works full time as a chef and shares her knowledge with readers on her blog, *Cindy's Recipes and Writings*. As an avid competitive cook, Cindy also participates in cooking contests held throughout the United States.

CPSIA information can be obtained
at www.ICGtesting.com
Printed in the USA
LVHW020045071119
636619LV00017B/204/P